The Monterey Peninsula

Text and Captions by Randall A. Reinstedt
Historical Photographs from the Pat Hathaway Collection
"Partners in Progress" by Raymond Mungo
Produced in Cooperation with the Monterey History and Art Association
Windsor Publications, Inc.
Northridge, California

The Monterey Peninsula

AN ENCHANTED LAND

Windsor Publications—History Book Division

Vice President, Publishing: Hal Silverman
Editorial Director: Teri Davis Greenberg
Design Director: Alexander D'Anca

Staff for *The Monterey Peninsula: An Enchanted Land*
Senior Editor: Jerry Mosher
Picture Editor: Laura Cordova
Editorial Development: Pamela Schroeder
Proofreader: Susan J. Muhler
Director, Corporate Biographies: Karen Story
Assistant Director, Corporate Biographies: Phyllis Gray
Editor, Corporate Biographies: Brenda Berryhill
Layout Artist, Corporate Biographies: Mari Catherine Preimesberger
Layout Artist, Editorial: Christina McKibbin
Editorial Assistants: Kathy M. Brown, Nina Kanga, Susan Kanga,
  Pat Pittman
Designer: Thomas Prager

Library of Congress Cataloging in Publication Data
Reinstedt, Randall A.
  The Monterey Peninsula.
  "Produced in cooperation with the Monterey History and Art
Association."
  Bibliography: p. 125
  Includes index.
  1. Monterey Peninsula (Calif.)--History. 2. Monterey Peninsula
(Calif.)—Description and travel. 3. Monterey Peninsula (Calif.)—
Industries. I. Mungo, Raymond, 1946- . II. Title.
F868.M7R45 1987 979.4'76 87-10673
ISBN 0-89781-199-2

Previous page: Perkins Park on Pacific Grove's rocky coast is named for Hayes Perkins, who moved near the Grove's shore in 1938. Perkins removed the shoreline's poison oak and replaced it with shrubs and colorful groundcover that he had observed during his worldwide travels. He died in 1964, but his work has been continued by the city and interested residents. Photo © 1987 George Elich

Facing page: Appropriately framed by the branches of a wind-swept cypress tree is the impressive Cypress Point clubhouse. This picture was taken from the vicinity of the 17th fairway in 1931. The clubhouse is situated on a knoll and commands a view of the Cypress Point Golf Course and the nearby Pacific. Photo by Louis Josselyn. Courtesy, Pat Hathaway Collection

Endsheets: Charles Gildemeister sketched this view of Monterey in the early 1840s. Several of the structures depicted in this lithograph are still a part of the city. Courtesy, The Bancroft Library

Contents

Foreword 6
Introduction 8
Acknowledgments 9

Chapter I
MONTEREY:
California's Historic First Capital
11

Chapter II
PACIFIC GROVE:
"God's Kingdom by the Sea"
41

Chapter III
CARMEL:
Paradise Among the Pines
63

Chapter IV
PEBBLE BEACH:
A Magnificent Meeting of Land and Sea
89

Chapter V
PARTNERS IN PROGRESS
99

Bibliography 125
Index 126

Foreword

"Monterey, as far as my observation goes, is decidedly the pleasantest and most civilized-looking place in California," wrote Richard Henry Dana, Jr., in his American classic *Two Years Before the Mast*. These words written in 1835 described the entire Monterey Peninsula and the yet-to-be-named towns described in this volume. Many of us feel that these words are as true today as they were in 1835. The Monterey Peninsula has a heritage which cannot be matched by any place in the state and by few places in the nation. With well-researched words and rare photographs, Randall A. Reinstedt and Pat Hathaway have created a rich resource which local residents, visitors, and "hope-to-be" visitors will find informative and thought provoking. It is written in an easy style and will be well received even by those individuals who "think" they don't like history. It will be some time before anyone produces a better local history.

Bob Reese
State Park Historian
Monterey State Historic Park
California State Department of Parks and Recreation

Mission San Carlos Borromeo del Rio Carmelo was founded in 1771 by Fray Junipero Serra, the father of California's mission chain, who died at the mission in 1784. After secularization the mission fell into disrepair in the mid-nineteenth century, but was restored in the 1880s and again in the 1930s. Today Carmel Mission has the rank of basilica and is a registered National Historic Landmark. Photo © 1987 George Elich

Introduction

The Monterey Peninsula, on California's rugged central coast, boasts one of the West's most colorful histories. At the hub of this beautiful headland is the bayside village of Monterey, perhaps best known to history buffs as California's first capital community. Adjoining Monterey on this picturesque promontory are the areas of Pacific Grove (established more than a century ago as a Methodist seaside retreat), Carmel (near the peninsula's south shore and home to one of the most historic and beautiful of all California missions), and Pebble Beach (nestled jewel-like along the Pacific and known to many as "The Golfing Capital of the World").

It is this enchanted land that this book is about. Beautiful to look at and delightful to visit, the Monterey Peninsula lends itself to an illustrated history as few areas do. Preserved on film by countless photographers, and collected from a vast variety of sources, the pictures presented on these pages provide a unique look at the Monterey Peninsula of yesterday, and offer a glimpse of the areas and their activities as they appear today.

In closing it is important to add that in a book of this format and size one can only briefly tell the story of this magical place. It is with this in mind that the author hopes the text and pictures found in this work will encourage its readers to further explore the Monterey Peninsula on their own, both through the excellent histories that have previously been written, and by visiting its beautiful and historic sites.

Randall A. Reinstedt

Above: The salmon troller Sarah *adds a picturesque touch to this east side view of Fisherman's Wharf. Courtesy, Pat Hathaway Collection*

Facing page: For the purposes of this publication, the Monterey Peninsula consists of the unshaded area within the curved line. Illustration by Mari Catherine Preimesberger

Acknowledgments

This book is dedicated to the many people who gave of their time and talent to help this publication become a reality. Singled out for work above and beyond the call of duty are Jessie Sandholdt, Mary Sherman, and Robert Reese. In addition to this talented trio are several other individuals who contributed in a variety of ways. Among those who deserve special thanks are: Margaret Adams, Jim Bajari, Alan Baldridge, Lee Blaisdell, Robert Blaisdell, Marabee Boone, Brooks Bowhay, Emily Brown, Martin Brown, Vincent J. Bruno, Dave Davis, Pat Fatchett, Allene Fremier, Wil Goodrich, Ruth Kelly, Florence Leideg, Frank Lloyd, Sudy Macdonald, Leslie Navari, Max Plapp, Otto Plapp, Carol Rissel, Beth Robinson, Dorothy Ronald, Rey Ruppel, Tom R. Russo, Tony R. Souza, Adam Weiland, and members of the Carmel Mission staff.

Numerous other individuals have also been involved in the publication of this work. It is with these people in mind that the author wishes to thank all who answered a question, checked a fact, loaned a photograph, shared a memory, and had an encouraging word to say along the way.

The author also wishes to mention that even though many people and sources were consulted, and countless hours were spent in checking and rechecking facts, discrepancies may appear as additional information becomes known. For this reason he apologizes for any mistakes that are found, or for any information that is misleading.

Finally, the Monterey History and Art Association is to be thanked for its interest and support. Without the sponsorship of this outstanding organization this book would not have been possible.

In closing, and perhaps of most importance, the author wishes to thank his wife, Debbie, and his son, Erick, for their continued encouragement and understanding.

Randall A. Reinstedt

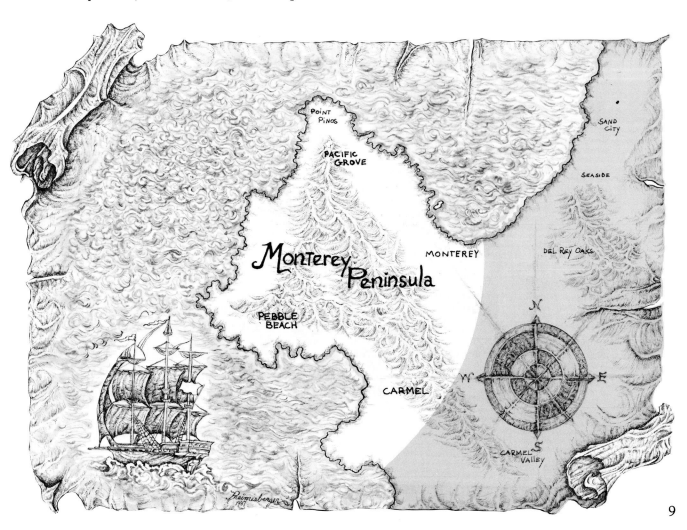

California's constitutional convention was held in September 1849 at Colton Hall. The building is named for Walter D. Colton, who arrived in Monterey in July 1846 and became the capital city's alcalde shortly thereafter. Colton used his influence, convict labor, money from the sale of town lots, fines from gamblers, and taxes from liquor shops to build a town hall. Upon its completion in March 1849, Colton Hall was described as California's "first public building of importance." Over the years it has been used as a school, an assembly hall, the Monterey County seat, headquarters of the Monterey Police Department, and the Monterey Municipal Court. Colton Hall is currently owned by the City of Monterey, and its downstairs section houses a variety of city offices. The upstairs portion is open to the public and has been restored to "the way it was" when the constitutional convention was held.
Photo © 1987 Lee Blaisdell

CHAPTER ONE

Monterey

CALIFORNIA'S HISTORIC FIRST CAPITAL

THERE IS CONSIDERABLE CONFUSION AS TO who was the first European to spot the Pacific promontory now known as the Monterey Peninsula. Various sources credit different explorers and early ship captains—some sources even claim the original sighting took place a mere 50 years after the Columbus voyage of 1492. However, it has been generally accepted that the first Europeans to plant the Spanish banner on the Monterey shore were men of the Sebastian Vizcaino expedition of 1602.

Vizcaino and his men also bestowed a name on the area. So impressed was the commander of this seventeenth-century exploration, and so sure that he had found a suitable harbor for the ships of the Pacific-circling Manila trade, that he honored the man responsible for his journey by naming the discovery after him. Because the Count de Monte Rey (the Viceroy of New Spain) sent Vizcaino on his coastal

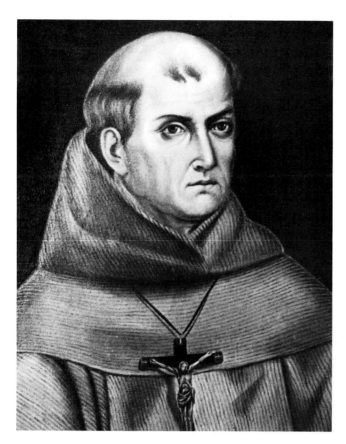

Above: Padre Junipero Serra founded 9 of Alta California's 21 coastal missions. Born at Petra, Majorca, Spain, in 1713, he died and was buried at Carmel's Mission San Carlos Borromeo del Rio Carmelo in 1784. This likeness of Father Serra was copied by Rev. Jose Mosqueda from a painting by an unknown artist, and is thought to show Serra as he appeared in his middle years. A copy of this painting hangs outside Serra's cell at the mission. Courtesy, Harry Downie Collection

Above right: Said to have been taken in the 1850s, this photograph is considered one of the earliest pictures of Monterey. Sources disagree on the identification of these buildings, but one can safely say that the large structure to the left is the Royal Presidio Chapel, one of Monterey's oldest and most important buildings. Courtesy, Pat Hathaway Collection

survey voyage, this beautiful bay and the site of Alta (Upper) California's future capital city became known as Monterey.

Unfortunately for Vizcaino, plans to build a harbor community on the shore of Monterey Bay were not acted upon for nearly 168 years. During this time the Monterey Peninsula continued to slumber, providing a home for California's coastal Indians. During the latter stages of this period, Russian fur hunters in search of sea otters made their way down the rugged Pacific Coast. Manila galleon captains observed the Russians and reported to Spanish officials, who decided that something must be done to show the Russians—and all others who cared to look—that Alta California was a part of Spain's far-reaching empire. Plans were thus formulated to settle the ports of San Diego and Monterey and to build a series of mission-oriented outposts along the coast.

The members of an exploratory expedition led by Captain Don Gaspar de Portola, Governor of Baja (Lower) California, reached the Monterey shores in September 1769 after an arduous overland trek from San Diego. However, when they looked out upon the waters of Monterey Bay, they did not recognize it as the secure and safe harbor Vizcaino had described so enthusiastically. Portola continued to lead his men in a northerly direction, discovering the beautiful bay of San Francisco. Portola and his men then realized they had gone too far—Monterey Bay was behind them. Retracing their steps, the Portola party again failed to recognize Monterey Bay and made camp on the south shore of the peninsula near Carmel Bay. Here the wanderers rested for more than a week while sending out scouting parties. Though the bay of Monterey was but a short hike from their camp, Portola and his men did not connect its rough and wind-blown waters with the sheltered harbor so generously described by Vizcaino in his 1602 diary.

They erected a cross near the Carmel Bay beach and another on the shore of the very bay they were seeking, each accompanied by a message indicating their plight and their lack of success. Portola and his party then began the long march back to San Diego.

In San Diego Portola discussed the findings and frustrations of the land expedition with an anxious Fray Junipero Serra, regional president of the Franciscan missions and founder of Alta California's famed mission chain. During this discussion, after checking all facts and previous descriptions, they decided Monterey Bay had in fact been found, but, because of Vizcaino's overenthusiastic reports, had not been recognized for what it was. They agreed on a second try. After rest, food, and treating of the sick, Portola and a crew of 16 soldiers set out once again for a march to Monterey Bay, with Father Serra to follow by sea.

Finally, on June 1, 1770, Serra, Portola, and members of the two parties met on the shore of the elusive bay. Two days later, near a great oak tree under which Vizcaino and his chaplain (Father Antonio de la Ascension) had performed mass nearly 168 years before, Serra performed a second mass and founded Mission San Carlos Borromeo, the second of California's 21 coastal missions. Portola raised the Spanish royal banner and—with ceremonial musket shots and cannon fire from the ship—founded the Presidio of Monterey. Thus was born a community destined to serve as Alta California's capital city for nearly three-quarters of a century. (Since the founding of Monterey took place in 1770, California's first capital city has the distinction of being older than the country of which it is now a part.)

Because of problems caused by soldiers and because of more fertile land and a better supply of fresh water near the mouth of the Carmel River (in the vicinity of Portola's 1769 encampment), Fray Serra chose in 1771 to move his church to the Carmel side of the Monterey Peninsula, the site it has occupied to this day. The California padre made his home there until he died in 1784. Known throughout the world as a man of God and the father of Alta California's famed Mission Trail, Padre Junipero Serra, perhaps more

than any other individual, brought early recognition to the Monterey Peninsula.

Early Monterey residents experienced many hardships, but as the years rolled on, word of the peacefulness and beauty of the north coast community began to spread. During Monterey's first 50 years of existence a few visitors from faraway lands found their way to the capital city and partook of its hospitality and happenings. Among the activities experienced by these travelers were horseback rides through the countryside, visits to the mission, and fiestas and fandangos at the homes and ranchos of California's fun-loving citizens. Outsiders were few during the early years, since California's ports were closed to foreign trade, but some of those who did arrive recorded their impressions in diaries.

The French nobleman Comte de la Perouse led a global voyage of scientific exploration to Monterey in 1786. He received a royal welcome and was treated to the best Monterey had to offer. Perouse left with words of praise for the country and its resources. Even though Perouse admired the flourishing mission, he had misgivings about the way its neophytes (Indians) were being treated.

In 1792 Captain George Vancouver sailed his British sloop into Monterey Bay. This representative of the British Royal Navy described the land as "lively" and "covered with an agreeable verdure." In light of what was to come it is also interesting to note that Vancouver was impressed with the capital city's lack of defenses, and he indicated that there would be little resistance should a "civilized nation" attempt to seize it.

A third foreign visitor of note to drop anchor near the capital city shore was Captain Ebenezer Dorr, who brought the first American ship into Monterey Bay. Unfortunately for Dorr and his crew, 1796 was not a good year for visitors. Fearing piracy (or perhaps conquest), the people of Monterey were wary of their guests and their star-spangled banner; their welcome this time was less cordial than most.

The Montereyans' fears of piracy were a bit premature, as it wasn't until 1818 that the first—and only—pirate arrived on the scene. One of the most dreaded of all Pacific pirates, the French privateer Hippolyte Bouchard left little to the imagination as he attacked and sacked California's capital city, taking what he wanted and burning much of what was left.

The San Carlos Cathedral was originally founded by Father Junipero Serra as the Church of San Carlos de Borromeo de Monterey (Mission San Carlos), on June 3, 1770. The following year, when Father Serra moved the mission to Carmel, the Monterey church became known as the Royal Presidio Chapel. Fire damaged the church beyond repair in 1789, and Manuel Ruiz, a Mexican master stonemason, supervised the building of a new church. He is thought to have carved the figure of the Virgin of Guadalupe (the Patron Saint of Mexico), located in a position of honor atop the church's facade. This statue is considered the oldest "indigenous" sculpture in California. The present Royal Presidio Chapel (seen here in the 1950s) was dedicated in 1795, and is located near the intersection of Church and Figueroa streets, within the area of Monterey's original presidio. The structure is an important part of old Monterey and serves as the community's main Catholic church. Photo © 1987 Lee Blaisdell

Above: This 1842 watercolor depicting the city of Monterey was probably painted by one of the officers under Captain Thomas ap Catesby Jones, commander of the American fleet in the Pacific. Jones, under the impression that the United States and Mexico were at war, demanded the surrender of Monterey on October 19, 1842, and took the city the following day. In this view an American flag waves over the port, although a Mexican flag is seen to the right. Soon thereafter, convinced of his error, Jones took down the American flag and replaced it with that of Mexico, with full honors. Courtesy, New York Public Library

Left: The sea otter played an important part in Monterey's history by attracting Russian hunters to the Pacific Coast. Hearing of the Russians' presence, Spanish officials made plans to settle the ports of San Diego and Monterey and thus claim Alta California for Spain's empire. Organized hunting of the sea otter put the animal near extinction by the mid-1800s, but a few managed to survive out of view off Monterey County's rugged south coast. The sea otter made a public "comeback" in 1938, when a small herd was observed near the Bixby Creek Bridge. Today, thanks to state and federal laws, the sea otter is protected and can be seen along the peninsula's coast. Photo © 1987 Richard Bucich

About all that can be said for this dark period in Monterey history is that it made California's governor Pablo Vicente Sola, as well as his regiment of soldiers, very much aware that their fort on the hill (El Castillo) was of little use in repulsing an enemy attack. A half-hearted attempt at rebuilding and strengthening the bayside fort is said to have ensued.

During its first 50 years Monterey's growth was anything but spectacular, due in part to Spain's early foreign trade restrictions as well as the remoteness of the outpost. However, the period was filled with events of interest and accomplishment. One important event was the 1775 movement of the provincial capital from Loreto (Baja California) to Monterey in 1775. This resulted in considerable status and prestige for the Alta California community. Even more important to the early development of Monterey was the arrival of Juan Bautista De Anza the following year. Although De Anza had made his first visit to Monterey two years earlier (after having blazed a trail from Mexico to Alta California), it was his arrival in 1776 with colonists (including women and children) and livestock that helped the struggling bayside community to gain a firm hold.

In 1777 Monterey was named the capital community for both Alta and Baja California. With this added honor Monterey also gained a new governor, Felipe de Neve, thought by many to have been one of California's best Spanish governors. Among his most significant accomplishments was the development of a code of laws for the regulation of civic and military affairs. Locally, Neve made improvements to the Monterey Presidio, transforming the wood-and-earth structures into more permanent quarters of stone and adobe.

In 1794 Diego de Borica assumed the governorship of California. Borica is remembered for a variety of things, among them his progressive outlook. He is credited with helping Father Fermin Francisco de Lasuen (leader of the California mission movement from 1785 to 1803) establish five new churches. But Borica is remembered more by Montereyans for his flowery letters and his expressed love of the area. Borica described his California headquarters in the following terms:

To live much and without care, come to Monterey. This is the most peaceful and quiet country in the world; one lives better here than in the most cultured court of Europe. It is a great country with healthful climate, not too hot, not too cold, good bread, excellent meat, tolerable fish, and bonne humeur which is worth all the rest.

Although Borica may have been a bit extravagant in his praise, Monterey around 1800 entered a golden age. The presidio was well established; the Mission San Carlos shared in the glory years of the California mission system; new arrivals had added energy and excitement to the capital community; life was becoming considerably more settled (although people and places were still somewhat isolated); and a time of peace and tranquility was on the horizon. Unfortunately, this golden age of happiness and hospitality was not enjoyed by everyone. When the Spanish celebrated their fiestas and fandangos, California Indians more often than not took part in the activities as servants rather than participants.

In 1821 the ports of Monterey and San Diego were officially opened to foreign trade. This ruling did not initially increase trade to any great extent; during the latter stages of Monterey's first 50 years, local restrictions had been relaxed, and foreign vessels were welcomed for the duties they paid.

The following year the California territory experienced a change of government. After 300 years of rule from across the sea, Mexico gained its independence from Spain. When the Mexican flag was raised over Monterey, local residents reacted with mixed emotions. Some were concerned as to what would become of the capital city and the way of life to which they were accustomed. Others took up the chant *Viva la independencia Mexicana* (Long live Mexican independence) and enjoyed feasts and festivities, accompanied by church services and a gala ball.

Under Mexican rule the way of life in and around Monterey was to change. The missions became secularized, undermining the mainstay of early California life. Foreign trade traffic increased. Many Montereyans began searching for new ways to bring happiness and prosperity to their community.

The Mexican rulers made many more land grants than the Spanish had, and huge ranchos were carved from the expropriated mission holdings. The population of cattle far outnumbered that of people, and foreign ship captains showed a strong liking for dried

cowhides—"California bank notes." It was only natural that local residents would look to the fledgling hide and tallow trade to provide a new way of life. (Tallow came from the fat of the animals and was used to make candles and soap.)

Old records show that this new endeavor was quite profitable for many. Foreign ships (mostly English and American) arrived on a much more regular basis. California's cattle supply seemed to be limitless, and the economy of the community came to be based on the hide and tallow trade. Bartering became a way of life; manufactured goods, wearing apparel, and other needed commodities were traded for the prized California bank notes.

The new economic order ushered in a colorful period of Monterey history, in social life as well as in commerce. When a foreign ship arrived and the duties were paid at the custom house, the serious business of bartering began. Hides and tallow were piled high on the shore, brought to the beaches in ox-drawn carts. The residents excitedly boarded the vessels and inspected the goods. When the Montereyans decided on what they wanted, a bargain was struck and a trade was made. It was also a social event to board the ships

The Casa Estrada Adobe, on the west side of Tyler Street between Pearl and Bonifacio streets, was built as a two-story building in the 1820s by Don Jose Mariano Estrada, and served as the Estrada family home for many years. In 1849 the building became the St. Charles Hotel. In 1880 a third story was added (as seen here in the 1890s), and in 1900 an additional wing was put on, and the St. Charles became known as the Mission Inn. In 1961, after serving as a hotel for more than 100 years, the property was purchased by the Monterey Savings and Loan Association and was later restored to its pre-hotel days. Today its exterior appears as it did when it was the Estrada family home, and its interior is used for offices and small civic gatherings. Courtesy, Pat Hathaway Collection

and view the many items they had to offer. The ships' officers were often invited to fiestas and festivities at the ranchos and in the homes of wealthy Californians. Crew members of the trading vessels also enjoyed the hospitality of the time, and their trips to shore were eagerly awaited.

Adding much to the enjoyment of their guests' visits were the Montereyans' various forms of entertainment. The residents needed little reason to host a ball or participate in a gathering. Among the most popular events were dances, picnics on the beach and in the surrounding woods, receptions honoring important guests, all-night fiestas and fandangos, and the ever-popular rodeos, where the horseback riding skills

Known as El Cuartel (The Barracks), this rather elongated building of adobe and redwood was built in 1840 for use by soldiers of the "Monterey Company." In later years (during the American period) the building was the headquarters of the military governor. Scout Kit Carson also reportedly delivered messages here from Washington, D.C. Another claim to fame for this structure was its use by Walter Colton and Robert Semple for the publication of the first newspaper in California. The building also housed one of the first libraries and schools in the area. It was located on Munras Street (slightly south of present-day Simoneau Plaza) and was torn down in 1910. In the distance, at the end of the street, is the LaPorte building. Photo by Taber. Courtesy, Pat Hathaway Collection

of the California cowboy could be displayed. Among other events that always drew a crowd were bull and bear fights staged in specially prepared pits of old Monterey. The bull and bear fight was a unique and very bloody sporting event of Early California. The bear was a grizzly, and the bull was a carefully selected specimen from one of the neighboring ranchos. Restrained by lassos and riatas, the ferocious beasts were led into the pit. They were tied together, usually by a hind leg, in such a way that they had room in which to maneuver but not to escape. At the proper signal the riatas were thrown off, and the two combatants fought to the death.

Considering the warmth of the residents and the enviable California lifestyle, it was inevitable that men from the foreign trade vessels would forsake their homelands and seek opportunities in Monterey. Many adopted the religion of the area, became Mexican citizens, married into wealthy Spanish families, obtained large tracts of land, opened successful businesses, and became leaders in California affairs for years to come. Newcomers to California controlled the commerce of the coast and continued to welcome foreign traders and new arrivals to the area.

Notable among the accounts of Monterey during this period are the observations of Richard Henry Dana, Jr., a young man of New England upbringing who visited Monterey during the 1830s. Working as

a seaman aboard the hide and tallow ship *Pilgrim*, Dana took careful notes of everything he saw and eventually incorporated them into a book of his adventures, *Two Years Before the Mast* (1840). In describing Monterey, Dana states:

We came to anchor within two cables' lengths of the shore, and the town lay directly before us, making a very pretty appearance, its houses being of whitewashed adobe . . . red tiles too, on the roofs, contrasted well with the white sides and with the extreme greenness of the lawn, upon which the houses—about a hundred in number—were dotted about . . . There are in this place . . . no streets nor fences . . . so that the houses are placed at random upon the green. This, as they are of one story, and of the cottage form, gives them a pretty effect when seen from a

little distance . . . The Mexican flag was flying from the little square presidio, and the drums and trumpets of the soldiers, who were out on parade, sounded over the water, and gave great life to the scene . . . Monterey, as far as my observation goes, is decidedly the pleasantest and most civilised-looking place in California.

Monterey, however, was not always as serene as it would seem from Dana's description. The soldiers revolted over assorted matters; the seat of government was temporarily moved to San Diego; governors and military commanders engaged in rivalries and intrigue; a "foreign legion" was organized to protect the capital city; and there was a revolution of sorts, bringing Monterey's first "home-grown" governor to power. New foreigners continued to arrive, and many felt that California was destined for annexation, either by

Above: The Custom House, one of old Monterey's most important buildings, is California's first registered State Historical Landmark. It is also considered the oldest government building in the state, and perhaps west of the Mississippi. The American flag was first "officially" raised in California on the Custom House flagpole on July 7, 1846, after Commodore John Drake Sloat captured the city during the Mexican War. The building was originally used to collect custom fees (duties) from foreign shipping. Built in stages, the north section (seen here) was completed in 1827, the center section was built in 1841, and the south section was finished in 1846. Even though there was a major shift in California trade to the San Francisco area in the late 1840s, custom duties continued to be collected at Monterey until the 1860s. During the late 1800s the building began to fall into disrepair. Realizing the historic significance of the aged adobe, the Native Sons of the Golden West restored the structure to its original appearance in 1901. In 1929 the building first opened as a museum, and in 1938 it was purchased by the state. The building, seen here circa 1890, is located directly across from the entrance to Fisherman's Wharf. Courtesy, Pat Hathaway Collection

Left: The Soberanes Adobe, located at 336 Pacific Street, was built in the 1840s by Rafael Estrada. In 1860 it was acquired by the Esequiel Soberanes family, and remained in their possession until 1922. Later in the 1920s the building was purchased by Ruben and Jean Serrano, who restored it to its original appearance. In 1941 William and Mayo Hayes O'Donnell purchased the property and in 1954 Mrs. O'Donnell presented the building to the state. This 1903 photograph shows the backside of the building; the wood extension was added in the 1860s to enclose the kitchen. Courtesy, Pat Hathaway Collection

Above: Gallant Dickinson and his family came to Monterey in 1847. Soon after their arrival, Dickinson, with the help of his son-in-law A.G. Lawrey (a stonemason of considerable talent), began construction of what is believed to be the first brick house in California. After the completion of only the first wing, gold was discovered in the Sierra Nevada and Dickinson headed for the Mother Lode. The house was abandoned, and in 1851 it and 60,000 bricks (molded and fired locally) were sold for $1,091. With the original two-story wing being of "adequate" size and situated near the wharf in the center of much activity, the structure proceeded to serve a variety of uses. Among the most popular was that of a Spanish restaurant. Today the building is owned by the state, and work is being done to preserve the structure. The First Brick House, located in Monterey's Heritage Harbor complex, is directly east of the historic Whaling Station. Courtesy, Pat Hathaway Collection

Right: Monterey alcalde Walter D. Colton (1797-1851) published California's first newspaper, the Californian, with his partner Robert Semple. Colton's diary, written during his three-year term as mayor (1846-1849), provided the basis for his book, Three Years in California, published in 1850. The book provides detailed accounts of Monterey life at mid-century. From Cirker, Dictionary of American Portraits, Dover, 1967

England or by the United States.

It became obvious that England and America (as well as other foreign powers) were interested in this "Pacific plum." Since the United States and Mexico were not on the friendliest of terms, it came as no great surprise to Montereyans to see two American men-of-war sail into the bay on October 19, 1842. The two warships anchored as close to the Monterey shore as safety would allow.

In command of the two vessels was Commodore Thomas ap Catesby Jones. Under the impression that the United States and Mexico were at war, and that he had successfully beaten the British to Monterey, Jones wasted little time in sending a message to California's governor, demanding that he surrender to the United States of America. Governor Juan Bautista Alvarado was no stranger to turmoil, having been brought to power through a revolution of his own. After checking with his military commander and learning that the fortifications "were of no consequence as everybody knows," Alvarado decided that it would be best to surrender.

Documents were drawn up and terms agreed upon, and Jones sent 150 marines and sailors ashore. At this time the Mexican garrison marched out of the fort, with colors flying and music playing, and gave up their weapons without a shot being fired.

Within a few hours of his successful conquest, Jones read "current communiques" found in Monterey and realized that a terrible mistake had been made. The United States and Mexico had not yet gone to war! Profuse apologies were offered, the Stars and Stripes were lowered, and the Mexican flag was raised. Monterey—and all of California—was restored to Mexican rule. So ended the occupation of 1842. About all that can be said for this event is that Monterey proved to be a prize easily obtained by any interested party.

The stage was thus set for an encore performance during the Mexican War. On July 7, 1846, for the third time in 28 years, the residents of Monterey witnessed the scene of their capital city being taken by an enemy force. As in Commodore Jones' rehearsal of less than four years before, Commodore John Drake Sloat of the United States Navy sent troops ashore and, without resistance, raised the Stars and Stripes over Monterey. This act brought approximately 600,000 square miles of Mexican territory under American rule.

The new flag was greeted with indifference by many Californians, who had become disenchanted with the misrule of the Mexican government. Most Montereyans were willing to give the new government a chance, but there were a few hot spots of rebellion. When these disturbances were quelled, the capital city settled down to a tranquil yet progressive existence.

Walter D. Colton, a graduate of Yale University and a United States naval chaplain, became the alcalde (mayor and/or chief magistrate) of Monterey. Among Colton's many accomplishments during his three-year reign (1846-1849) was the publication of California's first newspaper. Colton's partner in the publication of the *Californian* was a tall frontiersman from Kentucky named Robert Semple, who was soon to be elected president of California's constitutional convention. Colton is also credited with impaneling the first jury in California, introducing penal labor into the territory, and helping to start the first public library. Among many other Monterey events during Colton's reign was the establishment of the first school

in California under American rule, the opening of the first United States Post Office west of the Rockies, and the building of the first brick house in the territory.

Another valuable legacy of Walter Colton was his diary. Full of interesting and informative notes, the diary served as the basis for his book, *Three Years in California*, published in 1850. The following excerpt from the Colton diary gives us a colorful account of Monterey in the late 1840s, as well as some insight into the man who wrote it.

There are no people that I have ever been among who enjoy life so thoroughly as the Californians. Their habits are simple; their wants few; nature rolls almost every thing spontaneously into their lap. Their cattle, horses, and sheep roam at large—not a blade of grass is cut, and none is required. The harvest waves wherever the plough and harrow have been; and the grain which the wind scatters this year, serves as seed for the next. The slight labor required is more a diversion than a toil . . . They attach no value to money, except as it administers to their pleasures . . . Their happiness flows from a fount that has very little connection with their outward circumstances . . . Their hospitality knows no bounds; they are always glad to see you, . . . take a pleasure in entertaining you . . . and only regret that your business calls you away.

Colton is also remembered for building a town hall, described as "the finest and most pretentious building in all of California." The ground floor served as a school, and the second story was designed for public meetings. The stone building was constructed in part by convicts and was financed to a great extent by the sale of town lots, fines from gamblers, and taxes from liquor shops. The town hall was the scene of California's constitutional convention in 1849. Forty-eight delegates from various locations convened there on September 21, 1849. When they adjourned six weeks later the territory had the makings of a constitution, and less than a year later California became the 31st state. Colton's imposing stone structure stands to this day in the heart of old Monterey, and is known as Colton Hall.

While the Colton years brought a degree of progress and prestige to Monterey, they were also the years during which gold was discovered in the Sierra Nevada. People poured into California's famed

Above: The Chinese fishing village was located in the vicinity of today's Monterey Bay Aquarium, between the present-day landmarks of Monterey's Cannery Row and Pacific Grove's Hopkins Marine Station. Home for several hundred Chinese, the village was thriving by the late 1800s, but was destroyed by a fire of suspicious origin in 1906. Its main street is seen here around the turn of the century. Courtesy, Pat Hathaway Collection

Above right: This outdoor shrine was located near the heart of the fishing community, and Chinese fishermen are said to have come to this sacred place to pray for a safe voyage. Photo by C.K. Tuttle. Courtesy, Pat Hathaway Collection

Mother Lode, and San Francisco and Sacramento became the gateways to the gold field. Monterey soon lost its capital city status and began a well-deserved siesta.

Many Monterey men joined the frantic rush for gold, but the old capital did not become a ghost town. Among happenings of note during the 1850s was the beginning of Monterey's whaling industry. Whales by the hundreds were often sighted in California's coastal waters, and exaggerated reports stated that "Whalers could fill up" while lying at anchor in Monterey Bay. It seemed only natural that whaling would someday become part of the local economy. In 1854 Captain J.P. Davenport organized a whaling company. His men, as well as others who were to follow, were known

as "shore whalers" because the whales they caught were brought to shore, where the blubber was rendered for oil. The success of whaling drew others to the area, and competing companies were soon formed. By 1861 there were four whaling companies operating in Monterey Bay. Many of the whalers were Portuguese, who added another ethnic element to the community. Unfortunately for the whalers the prosperity didn't last, partly because of a decline in the number of whales that visited the coast. After 1880 relatively little whaling was done at Monterey (except for a short revival in the late 1890s).

Other interesting arrivals from distant lands were the Chinese. Chinese workers from the Mother Lode began arriving in Monterey in the mid-1800s, and in later years ex-railroad workers followed. According to a San Francisco publication of 1853, a fishing village of between 500 and 600 Chinese existed on the shore of Monterey Bay. Many historians feel that this report was exaggerated, but it does serve as proof that many Chinese were in the area. Their fishing village continued to grow near the north shore of what is now Cannery Row. To some it was an eyesore, but to others it was "a quaint little town with narrow streets and crooked paths, a town with honest people and open doors." By 1888 the community was quite well known; a report by the United States Commission of Fish and Fisheries described it as "one of the most thriving settlements of its kind on the West Coast." Unfortunately, this picturesque village of dragons and joss houses was destroyed in 1906 by a fire of suspicious origin.

The 1870s marked the centennial of the community of Monterey, 100 eventful years of growth, progress, excitement, prosperity, and also decline. During its first 100 years, Monterey laid claim to a number of California "firsts." Among its more obvious honors is the distinction of being California's first capital. Monterey was also the first California community to have been attacked and sacked by a pirate, the first California town to have been taken by the United States, the birthplace of California's first newspaper (printed on California's first printing press), the meeting place of California's first jury, the host of the state's constitutional convention, and the site of California's first public building (the Custom House), post office, theater that charged admission, brick house, and public library. Monterey's first 100 years also saw the establishment of the first convent in California, the first proper hotel in the territory (The Washington), and the first pier in California (1845). Monterey staged California's first general election in 1822. Also in Monterey were the first frame house (built of ironwood shipped from Australia), the first private residence with an indoor fireplace, the first piano (shipped around the Horn in 1843), and one of the first billiard tables (which added considerably to the popularity of California's first hotel). The state's first weathervane adorned an early Monterey building that became known as the House of Four Winds, which is also recognized as the site of California's first hall of records.

An important figure in that century of firsts was a pioneer Montereyan by the name of Thomas Oliver Larkin. He arrived in Monterey in 1832 and became one of California's most respected and influential foreign residents. Among his many honors, Larkin was the first United States consul in California; his policies are credited with helping prepare the way for America's annexation of California. Larkin is also credited with establishing California's first nonmilitary hospital, arranging for the building of California's first wharf, and fathering Monterey's first "Yankee" child.

Larkin is also remembered for a house he built. The Larkin House, which stands to this day, is one of

Monterey's most prized buildings. The two-story adobe structure, complete with balcony, veranda, and walled-in garden, set the pattern for what was to become known as "Monterey architecture." Also known as "Monterey Colonial," this style combines Spanish, Mexican, American Colonial, and New England architectural features. (Adobe, for those unfamiliar with early California buildings, is sun-dried mud or clay brick; the term can also be used to describe a structure built this way: "the Larkin adobe.")

In the 1870s, Monterey began a second eventful century. In 1874 California's first narrow-gauge railroad was completed, primarily intended to haul agricultural freight from the valley community of

Constructed in the mid-1840s, the First Theater was built by Jack Swan as a boarding house and barroom for sailors, but Swan soon converted it to a theater at the request of nearby soldiers who wanted to put on a series of plays. With a makeshift stage, an orchestra of four, and plank-and-box seats, the soldiers staged Putnam The Iron Son of '76, considered to be the first dramatic performance to which an audience paid admission in California. With this performance, the building thus acquired its name. Shortly thereafter the soldiers were transferred, and the theater again became a boarding house. After serving a variety of uses, the structure was acquired by the state in 1906. In 1937, after a restoration campaign led by the Monterey History and Art Association, plays were again produced at the First Theater. Today the building remains an old-fashioned melodrama-type theater, and the "Troupers of the Gold Coast" give weekend performances. The building is open to visitors during the day, and is located on the southwest corner of Pacific and Scott streets. Courtesy, Pat Hathaway Collection

Above: Looking north on Calle Principal (known as Main Street in Monterey's early days), one sees The House of Four Winds. In the background are the Sherman Adobe and the Larkin House (with balcony). All of these buildings are still in existence and offer a delightful look at old Monterey. The House of Four Winds gained its name because it was the first building in Monterey to have a weather vane. The building served as a residence, a store (operated by Governor Alvarado), and as California's first hall of records. The adobe structure was built about 1830, and in 1914 it was purchased by members of the Monterey Civic Club—an organization to which it still belongs. The Sherman Adobe was built in 1834 by Thomas O. Larkin and is located within the yard of the Larkin House. From 1847 to 1849, Lieutenants William T. Sherman and Henry W. Halleck shared its quarters before going on to become generals during the Civil War. Courtesy, Pat Hathaway Collection

Right: The Larkin House set the pattern for what was to become known as "Monterey architecture" and/or "Monterey colonial." The house was built in the 1830s by Thomas Oliver Larkin, one of California's most respected and influential foreign residents. In the mid-1840s Larkin served as U.S. consul to Mexico, and his home became the consulate. Walter Colton also used one of the rooms as his office during his reign as alcalde. During this period the Larkin House was considered the center of social life in the capital city. In 1922 the adobe was purchased by Larkin's granddaughter, Mrs. Alice Larkin Toulmin, who lived in the structure for 35 years. In 1957 she presented the house (complete with its antique furnishings) and its adjoining gardens to the state. Today the house is open to the public on a guided tour basis. It is located on Jefferson Street, between Calle Principal and Pacific Street. Courtesy, Pat Hathaway Collection

Salinas, 19 miles inland, to the port of Monterey, where it could be loaded aboard ships for its final destination. Unfortunately, the line never became the success that its backers had envisioned. Financed by local investors, including Monterey County land baron David Jacks, the "short-lived shortline" was known as the Monterey and Salinas Valley Railroad. (It brought Monterey's second wharf into being; the railroad's "Depot Wharf" was constructed in 1874, and a portion of it was in use for such things as fishing until 1940.) In 1879 the railroad succumbed to the mighty Southern Pacific, which at the time was controlled by the Central Pacific Railroad. With the Monterey Peninsula all to itself, the Southern Pacific wasted little time in laying a standard-gauge line to Monterey.

In 1875 a neighboring community was founded on the peninsula's north shore. Known today as Pacific Grove, it began as a Methodist seaside retreat. This community brought numerous people to the peninsula and was enthusiastically described as "God's Kingdom by the Sea." (For a more complete history of this area, see the Pacific Grove section of this book.)

In the same year that Pacific Grove had its beginning, south Monterey County's Los Burros Mining District was founded. Although gold had been mined in the Santa Lucia Mountains for many years, it wasn't until 1875 that the gold seekers felt it necessary to establish an official district to ensure mining justice. With law and order of sorts prevailing, and with the cry of "Gold!" in the air, Monterey enjoyed a minor gold rush in its own back yard.

In 1879 Monterey was visited by a lanky gentleman from Scotland who had traveled thousands of miles to be with his lady love. He was impoverished,

exhausted, and gravely ill while in Monterey, and he stayed for only a few months, but he left behind a description of the town that has delighted historians for more than a century. The visitor was author Robert Louis Stevenson (then little known), and the following excerpt from his work "The Old Pacific Capital" gives us a glimpse of the Monterey he knew:

Spanish was the language of the streets . . . A weekly public ball took place with great etiquette, in addition to the numerous fandangoes in private houses . . . Night after night serenaders would be going about the street, sometimes in a company and with several instruments and voices together, sometimes severally, each guitar before a different window. It was a strange thing to lie awake in nineteenth-century America, and hear the guitar accompany, and one of these old, heart-breaking Spanish love songs, mount into the night air, perhaps in a deep baritone, perhaps in that high-pitched pathetic womanish alto which is so common among Mexican men, and which strikes on the unaccustomed ear as something not entirely human but altogether sad.

Several Montereyans felt a sadness of their own when it was time for Robert Louis Stevenson to leave, for he had made a number of friends. Stevenson himself left in better health and good spirits; he was soon to marry Fanny Osbourne, the lady who had attracted him to the peninsula in the first place.

In the 1880s, Monterey became a playground for the rich, a place to see and be seen for the wealthy of the world. It all started with a visit to Monterey

Above: The Robert Louis Stevenson House, named after the author who once lived there, was constructed in the 1830s. It was originally owned by Don Rafael Gonzales (the first appointed collector of the port in Monterey), who sold the adobe to a Frenchman, Juan Girardin, in 1856. After a variety of changes were made, rooms were rented and the building became the French Hotel. It was known by this name when Stevenson stayed there in 1879, and during this period the hotel catered to the "Bohemian" set. The original structure, seen here circa 1910, has served many uses over the years, including that of a tinsmith shop and a carriage factory. Today it is owned by the state and is open for tours featuring Stevenson memorabilia and period furniture. It is located on Houston Street, between Pearl and Webster streets. Photo by Louis Josselyn. Courtesy, Pat Hathaway Collection

Left: Looking north down Alvarado Street in the early 1880s: The most notable (and perhaps only) structure that remains is the LaPorte building on the extreme left. Originally a one-story adobe, it was used for offices by Juan Bautista Alvarado (for whom Monterey's main street was named) before he became California's governor in 1836. In 1855 Alvarado acquired the structure. In 1874 the LaPorte brothers purchased the property and added a frame second story, and the building became known as LaPorte Hall. The building was completely renovated in 1936, and a small auditorium was added upstairs. Today the structure houses a bank as well as several offices. The large bay-windowed, false-fronted building to the right of LaPorte Hall was known as the White House, a dry goods store and long-time Monterey landmark. Photo by C.W.J. Johnson. Courtesy, Pat Hathaway Collection

in 1879 by Charles Crocker, one of California's "Big Four" railroad barons. (The others were Leland Stanford, Mark Hopkins, and Collis P. Huntington.) Crocker was charmed by Monterey and thought it the perfect place to build a seaside resort. He purchased 7,000 acres of choice real estate from David Jacks, a Scotsman who came to Monterey in 1850 and became one of the wealthiest landowners in the county. The Pacific Improvement Company, controlled by the Big Four, took title to the land and set out to develop a luxurious resort. This marked the beginning of a Monterey Peninsula industry that to this day is of major importance to the economy and prestige of the area: tourism.

No expense was spared. A majestic hotel soon rose from a miniature forest of oak and pine approximately one mile to the east of old Monterey. Built at a cost of one million dollars in a span of 100 days, the world's most elegant seaside resort opened its doors in June 1880. The grand spa was christened Hotel Del Monte and was soon the talk of the land. Trains such as the Del Monte Express, the Southern Pacific's oldest name train, made daily trips from San Francisco to the hotel, where colorful tallyhos (coaches) and elegant horse-drawn carriages met the arriving guests at the Del Monte Station. Publicized as the "Queen of American Watering Places," the splendid castle-like structure more than lived up to its billing. It began attracting the rich and famous from all over the globe.

The outside was pearl gray in color, and the interior was a rich, creamy white. There were lavish chandeliers and thickly carpeted hardwood floors. The parlors and sitting rooms featured colorful tapestries and massive fireplaces. On the long arcades and inviting verandas, delighted guests strolled in fashionable attire. Among the amenities unusual in 1880 were a telephone and hot and cold running water in each room—even those on the top floor. All fur-

The Hotel Del Monte, before the fire of 1887 destroyed it, was a Victorian castle of "Swiss-Gothic" design. It was the brainchild of Charles Crocker, one of California's "Big Four" railroad barons who counted among their holdings the Pacific Improvement Company, overseer of the Hotel Del Monte. Constructed at a cost of one million dollars, this elegant edifice was built in just 100 days, opening in June 1880. Located only a short distance from downtown Monterey and an even shorter distance from the Monterey beach, the hotel attracted visitors from throughout the world and was considered an "overnight success." The construction of this hotel is credited by many as the beginning of the Monterey Peninsula's tourist industry. Photo by C.W.J. Johnson. Courtesy, Pat Hathaway Collection

nishings were in the best of taste, and the dining room (including service, cuisine, and decor) was of the highest quality.

As the park-like grounds blossomed and the setting became even more beautiful, the Del Monte's fame and prestige continued to grow, until a disastrous night in 1887. As the majority of the guests slumbered on the night of March 31, a fire broke out at the Del Monte. Within a short time flames engulfed the wooden structure, and by morning there was little left but ashes and memories. Fortunately, no lives were lost in the conflagration. The rubble was cleared away, and plans for a larger and even more elaborate building began to take shape.

Within less than a year a new Hotel Del Monte graced the Monterey landscape. The 1888 version was of similar architecture but was considerably larger and even more imposing than its predecessor. The hotel buildings covered more than 16 acres, and the dining room alone boasted four fireplaces and a seating capacity of 750 people. The new Del Monte contained rooms for 700 guests, as compared to facilities for fewer than 500 in the original structure. Its public rooms and gathering places were also larger and even more elegantly appointed.

The Del Monte led the way as the Gay Nineties

Counted among the Hotel Del Monte's "extras" was its bathing pavilion located on the nearby beach. Described as the largest facility of its kind in the world, this beach-side bathhouse boasted 210 dressing rooms and four 70-by-170-foot swimming tanks, three of which were heated to different temperatures, enabling one to prepare for a dip in the chilly surf by moving from pool to pool. In this 1887 photograph, bathing enthusiasts sport the costumes of the day. A fire "of undetermined origin" destroyed the bathing pavilion in 1930. Photo by C.W.J. Johnson. Courtesy, Pat Hathaway Collection

approached. Not content to have the most talked-about accommodations in the land, the hotel management also wanted the outdoor facilities to be without equal. Once again money was no object, and the already outstanding hotel grounds soon became a showplace beyond compare. The hotel grounds added to the prestige of nearby Monterey with several more California "firsts." The Del Monte Golf Course (which is played to this day) is the oldest golf course in the West, and the polo field and horse race track were also the first in California.

"Automobilists"—sportsmen of the horseless carriage crowd—found special accommodations at Del Monte. Other recreational facilities included

Above: Frank Booth and his vision of canning sardines started Monterey on the road to becoming "The Sardine Capital of the World." In this early photograph the fishing boat Thad *and its lighter (tow boat) float alongside the Booth Cannery pier. A portion of what would later be known as Fisherman's Wharf can be seen in the background. Photo by F.C. Swain. Courtesy, Pat Hathaway Collection*

Right: In the early days—before the sardine became king—the area now known as Cannery Row was a picturesque coastline dotted with sandy beaches and rugged outcroppings of rock. The largest structure to be found along its shores was known to locals as the Murray mansion. The main house was originally built by Hugh Tevis and was later acquired by David Jacks, who sold it to James Murray in 1904. As the estate continued to expand it eventually occupied 1,000 feet of waterfront and boasted several buildings, including a guest house with two suites of rooms, a bowling alley (which was converted into a picture gallery), a hot house, and a stable. In 1941, when members of the Murray family sold the buildings and grounds, the estate was practically surrounded by fish canneries and reduction plants. Courtesy, Pat Hathaway Collection

perfectly manicured lawn tennis courts, a half-mile maze of carefully cropped hedges, an immaculately maintained stable and carriage house, a picturesque 15-acre lake, archery ranges and croquet courts, miles of walking paths, exotic gardens, a popular beachfront bathing pavilion, and nearby boating and fishing facilities. The Del Monte also opened the beautiful Seventeen Mile Drive, where as many as 50 coaches made three daily trips around the peninsula's scenic southwest shore. It is not difficult to understand why the Hotel Del Monte was often referred to as "America's Most Loved Resort."

People of wealth, rank, and title continued to make up its clientele, and its calendar was filled with noteworthy events. The countless social activities included grand balls, gala parties, dazzling receptions, and extravagant group outings to the Seventeen Mile Drive. The hotel also gained considerable fame for its sporting events. Its polo matches attracted outstanding players from throughout the nation; its golfing contests fathered the California State Amateur Golf Championships. At the Del Monte tennis matches, the idea for Davis Cup competition is rumored to have begun. Its automobile races featured the likes of Barney Oldfield.

By the turn of the century, the Hotel Del Monte was making Monterey world famous. The 1900s dawned on the bay with great promise: a second major industry was about to be born, giving Monterey a new and colorful way of life and additional fame. Though not nearly as glamorous as the Del Monte, the sardine

fishing industry brought Monterey into the twentieth century and proved a boon to the people of the peninsula. When the fishing industry went into high gear, Monterey became known as "The Sardine Capital of the World."

Frank E. Booth, a frequent visitor to Monterey around the turn of the century, is credited with founding the local fishing industry. During his early visits to Monterey, Booth had been impressed with the number of sardines in the bay. Booth and his father were involved in canning salmon in their Pittsburg (California) plant, and Booth began to ponder the possibility of canning the abundant Monterey Bay sardine. He moved to the bayside community, founded the F.E. Booth Company, and built his plant near the Monterey wharf. This marked the beginning of Monterey's sardine industry.

Booth had help from Knute Hovden, a Norwegian immigrant and expert in fish packing, and Pietro Ferrante, a native of Italy who redesigned the Mediterranean-style lampara net for use in the deep waters of Monterey Bay. The company flourished and became quite successful, and Booth encouraged Ferrante to invite his Italian fishing friends to join in the hunt for sardines. Many of Ferrante's friends and relatives did find their way to Monterey, and their skills as fishermen ensured success for the sardine industry.

Also around the turn of the century, a new settlement began to grow near the peninsula's south shore. Situated on beautiful Carmel Bay, and a short walk from Father Serra's historic church, the hillside hamlet was dubbed "the Village" by people on the peninsula. As time went on, more and more people discovered its charms, and the quaint seaside community became known as Carmel. Artists, authors, and the Bohemian set were attracted to this town, which has since gained international fame. (For additional information see the Carmel section of this book.)

In 1910 Alvarado Street had a modern look: The streetcar line of the early 1890s had been electrified and became known as the Monterey and Pacific Grove Street Railway and Electric Power Company. As evidenced by the horseless carriages parked along the street, horse-drawn wagons were slowly giving way to the automobile. Photo by L.S. Slevin. Courtesy, Pat Hathaway Collection

Above: After the 1924 fire the Hotel Del Monte was again rebuilt. As it rose from the ashes for the second time it took on a Spanish (and/or Mediterranean) design. Having learned from the past, the new Del Monte was described as fireproof as well as earthquake proof. The wings were renovated and the overall edifice was larger and even more palatial than its predecessor. Today the hotel building looks much the way it did when this photo was taken in 1929. The aged building is now the headquarters of the United States Naval Postgraduate School, known to many as "the Annapolis of the West." Photo by Louis Josselyn. Courtesy, Pat Hathaway Collection

Right: Hotel San Carlos employees show off their Spanish attire during the 1928 Serra Pageant, an annual Monterey celebration honoring Father Junipero Serra. At the time this picture was taken, the Hotel San Carlos was one of the largest and most popular peninsula hotels, featuring rooms with beautiful views of the bay. Perhaps the most popular of its attractions was the Skyroom, located atop the nine-story structure. From the Skyroom "big band" music echoed throughout the town as couples danced on a floor mounted on springs. This Monterey landmark "officially" closed its doors in December 1981. The San Carlos was demolished in 1983, and today the 338-room Monterey Sheraton Hotel stands on the site. Courtesy, Pat Hathaway Collection

Monterey's fishing industry continued to grow. By 1916 fishing and canning techniques had come of age and the fishing fleet was larger and more accomplished, so Knute Hovden decided it was time to branch out on his own. His cannery, built on the dividing line between Monterey and Pacific Grove, helped set the stage for Monterey's future cannery development. One cannery after another was built on this scenic stretch of coast—known today as Cannery Row. From the 1920s into the early 1940s, canneries continued to be built, fish continued to be caught, and much of Monterey was supported by the sardine. Although other important events took place on the peninsula, the sardine remained king. The stench of fish that drifted throughout the area, combined with "outlandish odors" from the fish reduction plants, was the sweet smell of prosperity for many people on the peninsula.

Among the other events of importance during this period was the sale in 1919 of the Hotel Del Monte and the vast acreage that went with it. Fortunately for residents of the peninsula, the package was purchased by the Del Monte Properties Company. This newly

In addition to a small Monterey police building, facing Calle Principal and located on the Monterey Sheraton Hotel block, this 1905 picture shows a number of historic and interesting buildings. The church with the high steeple, constructed around 1890, was a Presbyterian church for many years. In 1914 it was moved to another site to make room for a new and more adequate church building. To the left of the church across Franklin Street is Capitular Hall, originally constructed in 1834 as a one-story adobe. A second frame story was added at a later date, and for a time the building is believed to have been used as a town hall. In 1848 Walter Colton purchased the building for three ounces of uncoined gold. Today the building is privately owned and is used for offices. The large building behind Capitular Hall was the Freeman Undertaking Parlor, and has since been removed. To the right of the Presbyterian church is the two-story Merritt Adobe, built in the 1830s. The building is now restored and is part of a downtown "country inn" complex. Continuing in a northerly direction on Pacific Street is the small St. James Episcopal Church, built in 1874 as the first Protestant church in Monterey. In the late 1960s the church was to be razed as part of urban renewal, but the Monterey History and Art Association saved the building, moving it to a site overlooking Monterey harbor. Today the building is the Association's Mayo Hayes O'Donnell Library. Courtesy, Pat Hathaway Collection

organized company was headed by Samuel F.B. Morse, a young and imaginative individual dedicated to preserving the area's scenic beauty and bringing the Del Monte back to its original glory (which had faded somewhat in the years prior to the sale). The Del Monte regained its class and quality and again began attracting numerous visitors. All the communities of the peninsula benefited from the vacationers' renewed financial support.

In 1924, however, a second major fire swept through the main building of the Hotel Del Monte. Undaunted, Morse and company rebuilt what was destroyed and refurbished what was left. On May 8, 1926, the hotel reopened its doors and welcomed 1,600 people to a gala dinner and dance. Incorporating a bit of Monterey history into its design, the new Del Monte boasted a Spanish or Mediterranean look, with red tiles on its roof. Even though it appeared out of place to those accustomed to seeing a gothic structure there, the new Del Monte soon caught on. Upon inspection, it was found to be even larger and more palatial than its predecessor.

Other construction was going on in Monterey in the mid-1920s. During 1925 and 1926 a second major wharf was added to the waterfront, extending approximately 1,700 feet into the bay. Municipal Wharf Number Two was built to serve as a cargo pier, among other purposes. Perhaps of even more importance to local residents was the fact that the new wharf relieved congestion in and around Monterey's original wharf. Wharf Number One had grown in size and use along with the growth of the sardine industry and had become known as Fisherman's Wharf.

As the 1920s wound down, the people of the peninsula prospered and looked forward to a profitable future. However, the fall of the stock market in 1929 clouded their optimism. Although the sardine industry continued to operate, helping Montereyans weather the Depression, the Del Monte never quite recovered from the crash. The elegant hotel remained open and continued to cater to the world's elite, but it wasn't long before the "Del Monte habit" became a thing of the past, as America's lifestyle changed.

In the midst of the Great Depression, one of Monterey's most important cultural organizations was founded. The Monterey History and Art Association can now claim more than a half century of success and

At the cannery packing tables, the headless and tailless fish were packed by hand into cans. Photo by G.A. Robinson. Courtesy, Pat Hathaway Collection

a current membership of about 2,000. This organization has helped the City of Monterey preserve many of its old buildings. Thanks in large measure to the association, Monterey has the distinction of having preserved more original adobes than any other California community. In a period of bulldozers and blasting caps, when progress usually meant tearing down and starting anew, founders of this organization and their successors realized the importance of Monterey's past and fought to preserve a bit of yesterday for the people of today and those of tomorrow.

By 1934 feelings of optimism and stability were gradually returning to the United States. The Monterey fishing fleet also gained stability when a breakwater was added to the waterfront that year. The

breakwater aided immeasurably in protecting the ever-increasing number of vessels that called Monterey home and took part in the hunt for sardines. By the late 1930s, Monterey's fishing fleet recorded annual catches in excess of 200,000 tons. During these years the tiny port city's total fish tonnage is said to have ranked third in the world.

In 1937 the other major industry on the peninsula, tourism, received a great boost: The spectacular coast highway was opened. Extending to Southern California by way of the beautiful Big Sur coast, the scenic highway opened the area to tourism on an even grander scale and brought additional fame to the Monterey Peninsula. The father of Highway 1 was Monterey's Dr. John L.D. Roberts, whose dream of a coastal link to the south began with his turn-of-the-century treks to the Big Sur wilderness to care for the sick and needy. Many considered his dream to be impossible, but on June 28, 1937, Dr. Roberts was

With the "Row" continuing to grow, it was not long before there were very few places where one could get a glimpse of the sea. Perhaps it was for this reason—as well as the fame John Steinbeck's novel Cannery Row brought to the street—that the city of Monterey officially changed the name of Ocean View Avenue . . . to Cannery Row. At the time this picture was taken in the mid-1940s, the Row was described as the busiest, most colorful, noisiest, most profitable, and certainly the smelliest street on the Monterey Peninsula. The overhead walkways that helped to make this street so unique were used primarily to transport the canned fish from the canneries to the warehouse. Photo by G.A. Robinson. Courtesy, Pat Hathaway Collection

Above: From the sea to the hold was a one-way trip for the sardine, as seen on the purse seiner City of Monterey. *Photo by G.A. Robinson. Courtesy, Pat Hathaway Collection*

Right: Lampara boats, as well as the more efficient half-ring boats, became outmoded with the introduction of a vessel bearing a name that at one time was almost synonymous with the name Monterey: the purse seiner. The popular boat took its name from the type of seine net it carried, which, when full of trapped fish, formed a purse. The largest of the purse seiners approached the 100-foot mark and carried nets capable of encircling a football field in width, dropping to a depth of more than 100 feet in the water. This new breed of boat was also capable of fishing hundreds of miles at sea and carrying between 140 and 150 tons of fish in its hold. With the purse seiner's introduction and the elimination of the lighter, sardine fishing in and around Monterey Bay took on an added dimension. In this view of the Monterey harbor looking south, one sees a number of these proud vessels, with an even prouder fishing community in the background. Photo by R. Ruppel. Courtesy, Pat Hathaway Collection

The opening of Monterey County's Highway 1 in 1937 greatly enhanced the peninsula's accessibility and popularity as a vacation destination. Among the route's most awe-inspiring sights was Bixby Creek Bridge (originally known as Rainbow Bridge), shown here under construction in May 1932. Upon its completion, this magnificent bridge stretched to a length of 714 feet, rose to a height of 285 feet above the sea, and contained 6,600 cubic yards of concrete. Photo by Louis Josselyn. Courtesy, Pat Hathaway Collection

an honored guest at the official ribbon-cutting ceremonies for the highway that is often called America's most scenic and awe-inspiring. (Dr. Roberts played an important role in several other local projects and was the founder of the community of Seaside.)

In 1939 the Monterey sardine industry achieved startling production figures. The fishing fraternity's importance to the local economy is evident from this account in the *Monterey Peninsula Herald* newspaper:

Monterey's sardine industry produced almost $8,500,000 worth of canned fish, oil and meal during the fishing season of 1939. And . . . more important perhaps to Monterey Peninsula people . . . the industry paid out a total of $2,354,066 to the 71 purse seiners operating here and another $1,921,033 to the more than 2,500 people who are employed in the canneries.

Among the thousands of people who made up Monterey's "fishing family" were representatives of many races and nationalities, including Austrians, blacks, Irish, Japanese, Norwegians, Portuguese, Slavonians, and Spaniards. However, the Italians continued to make up the majority of the fishermen; they added a colorful style and proud tradition to the waterfront scene.

The 1940s brought many changes to Monterey and its neighboring communities. During the early years of World War II, Monterey became very military-oriented. In 1941 a reception center for inductees was

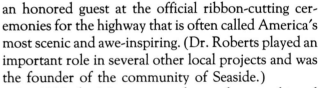

established at the Presidio of Monterey, which now occupied the site originally known as El Castillo. This spot boasted a sporadic military history dating back to California's earliest days. The "fort on the hill" had served a variety of uses, among them a United States Army cavalry post. While catering to the cavalry, the army decided that more space was necessary for training and began a search for additional land. In 1917 an agreement was reached with members of the Jacks family, and 15,809 acres of "sand dunes and scrub oaks" (located around the bay from the Presidio) became a maneuvering and training area for the army's horse soldiers.

This land eventually became known as Fort Ord. During World War II it was one of the United States' major training centers and grew by leaps and bounds. In 1942 the navy also arrived on the scene, signaling the end of an era for the peninsula. This era of Del Monte devotees and old world charm ended one year after America became actively involved in World War II, as the U.S. Navy took over the famed hotel. The opulent Hotel Del Monte became a pre-flight training facility, and the navy also became involved in the development of the Monterey airport. As the army and navy became increasingly important to the Monterey Bay area, many of the people on the peninsula enjoyed an added sense of security, as well as a boost in their income.

When the war was over, the army and navy stayed on. The Presidio became the Defense Language Institute; Fort Ord continued to expand; the Hotel Del Monte became the Naval Postgraduate School (often referred to as the "Annapolis of the West"); and the coast guard established a permanent station on the Monterey shore, providing aid to those in need along the treacherous central California coast. During and after the Second World War, when a vast number of military personnel and their families came to the area, the need for housing and services became acute. This need gave impetus to the expansion of several nearby communities; the towns of Seaside and Marina, which border Fort Ord, are two of the better known.

Now that the Hotel Del Monte no longer catered to the wealthy, S.F.B. Morse and company continued a preplanned development of the peninsula's opposite shore. Overlooking beautiful Carmel Bay, a "less pretentious" lodge had long before been built. This lodge, situated in the heart of picturesque Pebble

In this 1937 view of Wharf Number Two, one also sees one of Monterey's great community gatherings. In celebrating the end of a successful sardine season, happy boat owners and fishermen put on a banquet for the people of Monterey. Photo by R. Ruppel. Courtesy, Pat Hathaway Collection

Below: Monterey's Fisherman's Wharf, seen in this late 1920s view from the wharf's west side, has long been a favorite among visitors and residents alike. The structure to the left is a portion of the Booth Cannery complex. Photo by Louis Josselyn. Courtesy, Pat Hathaway Collection

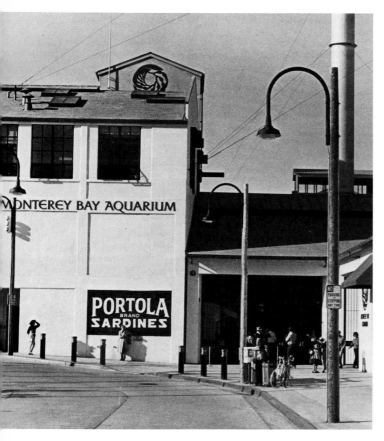

Above: The Monterey Bay Aquarium's exterior, rooflines, and overall architecture reflect those of the Hovden Cannery, which once stood on the site. While most of the construction is new, the old cannery's boilers have been restored as a museum display, complete with fiberglass smokestacks (upper right) to replace the old ones. The old warehouse (left) now houses the aquarium's offices, veterinary clinic, and divers' locker rooms. Portola Brand Sardines was just one brand packed by Hovden Cannery until the 1950s, when the sardines vanished from the bay. Squid, tuna, and other products were also canned. Finally, in 1972, the Hovden Cannery became the last on the old row to close. It was demolished in 1980, and aquarium construction began in 1981. Courtesy, Monterey Bay Aquarium

Facing page: The Monterey Conference Center opened in 1977, and its schedule of events keeps it busy throughout the year. This facility, and the thousands of visitors it draws, helps to stimulate the economy of the entire peninsula. In addition, the center hosts many events of interest to peninsulans and those in nearby communities. Courtesy, Monterey Conference Center

Beach, had gained its own measure of fame even before the end of the war. Surrounded by elegant homes, a beautiful golf course, and acres of trees, the lodge (and the accompanying Del Monte Forest) took over where the hotel had left off and became the peninsula's playground by the sea. (For more information on the southwest section of the Monterey Peninsula, see the Pebble Beach portion of this book.)

During the busy war years Monterey's fishing fleet continued to bring in record catches, and record prices were paid for its sardines. As was the case during World War I, the fish were especially valuable in wartime as a source of protein, and thousands of workers were hired to keep up with the demand. The peak year for Monterey's "fisher-folk" was 1945, but one might also say it marked the beginning of the end for the sardine industry. In 1946 the catch dropped considerably, and 1947 and 1948 showed even sharper declines. Except for the comeback years of 1949 and 1950, the sardine industry was soon to become a thing of the past. Canneries closed, purse seiners headed south where the fish were still plentiful, and the Montereyans who had depended on the sardine for survival began to seek other means of support. Various theories exist to this day as to the demise of the sardine: polluted waters, warmer climates, changing currents, recurring cycles, and the distinct possibility that the sardines were just plain fished out.

By coincidence, the year that marked the end of an era for the Monterey sardine industry also marked the beginning of a new era for the cannery-lined street where the fish were processed. During the sardine industry's peak year of 1945, Pulitzer and Nobel prize-winning author John Steinbeck, who was born in nearby Salinas, published Cannery Row. This book lent magic to the mile-long street, and it was not long before Steinbeck fans sought out the area in search of the color and characters of the old row. However, though the street reeked with atmosphere and the smell of fish, it was not the people-packed place that Steinbeck fans expected. Perhaps the disappearance of the sardine had changed forever the Cannery Row of Steinbeck lore, or maybe the frustrated newcomers were unable to find the mood or colorful characters that the master craftsman had created. Nonetheless, visitors continued to come, and before long the merchants of Monterey began to look toward the

silver spent by the tourists rather than the silvery sardine that for so many years had meant prosperity and security to the people of the peninsula.

It did not take long for the residents of this historic town to see that the future of the community was directly linked to its colorful past. The Monterey of the late 1940s and 1950s was transformed in the 1960s and 1970s, reoriented toward visitors and its own history. Cannery Row and Monterey's waterfront and downtown areas were reshaped into an array of elegant shops, gourmet restaurants, convention facilities, and restored buildings. Urban renewal became a subject of controversy, as a portion of Monterey fell to the bulldozer. The transformation of "lower Alvarado" (Monterey's main street near the waterfront) into an area oriented toward conventions and visitors was a painful process that opened gashes in the land and left bitterness among the people. The scars are now healed, and the bitter feelings have diminished. As Monterey celebrated its 200th birthday in 1970, its residents reminisced about an exciting and very proud past, but they also looked to the future with eager anticipation. Today the city and state are working together to make better use of Monterey's monuments and develop plans that will popularize its lovely and historic locations. Monterey boasts the largest collection of historic adobes in the state and is recognized as one of the most important historic sites in the West. It seems only fitting that a project of this type should take place here.

Just as two centuries ago, when the new town of Monterey eagerly welcomed newcomers to its Pacific shores, and just as 100 years later, when the grand Hotel Del Monte opened its doors to visitors from distant places, Monterey of the late twentieth century continues to cater to people from far and near. Long a vacation destination and home to many popular events, the visitor-oriented Monterey of today boasts a crowded calendar of conventions and attractive accommodations for thousands. Among the annual events in town are the Monterey Jazz Festival, the Commodore Sloat Landing Ceremony, the Santa Rosalia Festival, the Monterey Merienda, the Obon Festival, the Adobe Tour, the Monterey Wine Festival, the Dixieland Festival, the Cannery Row Reunion, the Great Monterey Squid Festival, and numerous sailing, fishing, and waterfront activities. These events, combined with the fabulous Monterey Bay Aquarium, and attractions and activities elsewhere on the peninsula, draw millions of visitors to the Monterey area each year. Such attractions help to make Monterey an exciting place to be. These events, along with the peninsula's scenic beauty, mild climate, and romantic history, make it easy to understand why most Montereyans are happy with today, and why they look forward to an even better tomorrow.

In the early days the Pacific Grove Retreat was protected
from outsiders, and all "modern" conveniences (which
some considered "a work of the devil"), by gates and a
fence. The entryway shown in this circa 1880 photo was
not open to vehicular traffic, providing access only for
those on foot. The gate was located near the intersection
of Lighthouse and Grand avenues, in the heart of present-
day downtown Pacific Grove. The buildings to the right
housed a small provisions store and restaurant, where
Ford's Department Store (formerly Holman's) is now located. The stout gentleman in the foreground is thought to
be J.O. Johnson, one-time superintendent of the Pacific
Improvement Company, and later the owner of the Mammoth Stable. Photo by C.W.J. Johnson. Courtesy, Pat
Hathaway Collection

CHAPTER TWO

Pacific Grove

"GOD'S KINGDOM BY THE SEA"

LIKE THE OTHER COMMUNITIES ON THE Monterey Peninsula, Pacific Grove has a unique personality. It is known for many things, including its beautiful shoreline, Monarch butterflies, and Victorian houses. History buffs probably know Pacific Grove best as a seaside retreat, a "piney paradise" that, over a century ago, was referred to as "God's kingdom by the sea." Its Point of Pines (Point Pinos) is the site of the West Coast's oldest continuously operating lighthouse, built in 1855 and still in use. The Point Pinos area has also been suggested as one of the landfalls described by the Portuguese explorer Juan Rodriguez Cabrillo. In 1542 while in the service of Spain, Cabrillo became the first European to sail up the rugged Alta California coast.

Even though Pacific Grove borders California's first capital city, its history is decidedly different. In 1873 Monterey County land baron David Jacks owned

Above: The Grove's 30-by-60-foot tent lots sold briskly, and it was not long before tent-like structures were built— some right over the existing tents! A number of the Grove's early rules were reflective of the tent culture, such as a ban against smoking on the platforms (tent floors). This rule was especially important since there was no fire department in the retreat's early days. Photo by C.W.J. Johnson. Courtesy, Pat Hathaway Collection

Below: Completed in 1855, the Point Pinos Lighthouse is considered the oldest continuously operating lighthouse on the West Coast. The main structure is built of granite quarried near the site. After the 1906 San Francisco earthquake damaged the tower, modifications were made to the structure, but the lighthouse still boasts the original lenses and prisms. The light source stands 89 feet above sea level, and when conditions are right it is visible from a distance of 15 miles. Courtesy, Pat Hathaway Collection

Facing page: This photograph was taken in 1879, the year Robert Louis Stevenson visited the "dreamlike" Pacific Grove Retreat. Stevenson described this outdoor minister's pavilion, where many of the retreat's early gatherings were held, as an "open-air temple, with benches and soundingboard." Photo by C.W.J. Johnson. Courtesy, Pat Hathaway Collection

much of the property that was to become Pacific Grove. In the summer of that year, Jacks granted permission to a Methodist minister to build a small house on his holdings. The Reverend Ross and his wife had exhausted all "modern" medicines in their search for relief from various ailments. They were advised to make their home in an area "where the fluctuations from heat to cold were merely nominal." After much research, they chose the Monterey Peninsula. After only a short time living "amongst the pines," they experienced a remarkable improvement in their health. With a new lease on life, Ross returned to his former home in the East and convinced his brother and sister-in-law (both of whom were suffering from pulmonary problems) to return with him to his pine-forested promontory. Settling in what is now Pacific Grove, the four of them ignored most indoor comforts and lived primarily on fish and game. They looked upon the improvement in their health as almost miraculous.

Rev. Ross entertained many visitors at his woodsy residence, and word of the benefits of his peaceful grove soon spread. Among his more distinguished guests was the Methodist bishop Jesse Truesdale Peck, a member of a group of Methodist clergymen who had been seeking a suitable California site to build a church summer camp. They needed an atmosphere conducive to religious meetings, for they wanted to establish a Christian seaside retreat similar to the one in Ocean

Grove, New Jersey. Peck's stay with Rev. Ross in 1874 led him to convince the others on the committee that he had found just the place they were seeking. The Pacific Grove Retreat Association was founded at a meeting in San Francisco on June 1, 1875.

When he heard about the project, David Jacks generously advanced a large sum of money and contributed 100 acres of prime land—a portion of downtown Pacific Grove now stands on part of this property. The bayside retreat got off to a fast start. In August 1875 the first in a long line of camp meetings was held. As the years rolled on, the fame of the Pacific Grove Retreat spread far and wide, drawing an ever-increasing number of people to the religious resort.

Visitors described this Methodist meeting place as "a little paradise," a place to "breathe the pure aroma of the pines" and "inhale the ozone from the broad Pacific." Its climate was said to be "the most equable

in the known world," "so healthy that doctors scarely make a living." Such descriptions induced even more people to visit the Grove, hoping to cleanse their bodies as well as their souls.

During the early years of the retreat, most of the activities took place during the summer season. Meetings were usually held outdoors or under a huge tent. Smaller tents served as accommodation for many of the people who attended the gatherings. The sale of 30-by-60-foot "tent lots" was brisk, and some came to look upon the Grove as a real estate venture. Soon small houses were built on the tiny lots, a limited number of stores opened their doors, and straight streets were laid out. Before long the Grove became a haven for conventions, catering to such groups as the Young Men's and Young Women's Christian Associations, the State Sabbath School, the Women's Christian Temperance Union, and (perhaps most important) the Chautauqua Society. The Chautauqua organization began in 1874 at Lake Chautauqua, New York, as a summer training camp for Methodist Sunday School teachers. Chautauqua developed into a nationwide cultural and educational movement, featuring entertainment, concerts, lectures, and readings. In 1879, Chautauqua arrived at the Pacific Grove Retreat. At first the gatherings were held in temporary quarters, including a large tent. In 1881 the meetings were moved to a new wood building that is a Pacific Grove landmark to this day and is known as Chautauqua Hall.

When Robert Louis Stevenson lived on the Monterey Peninsula in 1879, he visited the Point Pinos lighthouse. On the way there, he happened on the Pacific Grove Retreat, which was all but deserted in the off-season. Stevenson's description of this Methodist campground is one of the best that we have.

One day—I shall never forget it—I had taken a trail that was new to me. After awhile the woods began to open, the sea to sound nearer at hand. I came upon a road, and, to my surprise, a stile. A step or two farther, and, without leaving the woods, I found myself among trim houses. I walked through street after street, parallel and at right angles, paved with sward and dotted with trees, but still undeniable streets, and each with its name posted at the corner, as in a real town. Facing down the main thoroughfare— "Central Avenue" as it was ticketed—I saw an open-air temple, with benches and sounding-board, as though for an orchestra. The houses were all tightly shuttered; there was no smoke, no sound but the waves, no moving thing. I have never been in any place that seemed so dreamlike. Pompeii is all in a bustle with visitors, and its antiquity and strangeness deceive the imagination; but this town had plainly not been built above a year or two, and perhaps had been deserted over-night. Indeed, it was not so much like a deserted town as like a scene upon the stage by daylight, and with no one on the boards. The barking of a dog led me at last to the only house still occupied, where a Scotch pastor and his wife pass the winter alone in this empty theater. The place was "The Pacific Camp Grounds, the Christian Seaside Resort." Thither, in the warm season, crowds come to enjoy a life of teetotalism, religion and flirtation, which I am willing to think blameless and agreeable. The neighbourhood at least is well selected. The Pacific booms in front. Westward is Point Pinos, with lighthouse in a wilderness of sand, where you

will find the light-keeper playing the piano, making models and bows and arrows, studying dawn and sunrise in amateur oil-painting, and with a dozen other elegant pursuits and interests to surprise his brave, old-country rivals.

The resort also attracted people bent on leisure activities of a wilder sort than worship. To combat these influences, the leaders of the Christian retreat (and in later years the elected officials of the town) enacted a code of blue laws. In the eyes of some observers, Pacific Grove remained an outpost of Puritanism well into the twentieth century. One ordinance read:

It shall be unlawful for every person wearing a bathing suit or portion thereof, except children under the age of ten years, to appear in or upon the beach or in any place open to the

This scene of perhaps a century ago depicts one of the Grove's earliest homes, as well as a number of carefully posed and very obliging residents and visitors. Photo by C.W.J. Johnson. Courtesy, Pat Hathaway Collection

public—unless attired in a bathing suit or other clothing of opaque material, which shall be worn in such a manner as to preclude form. All such bathing suits shall be provided with double crotches or with skirts of ample size to cover the buttocks.

It was further stated:

Bathing without costumes, or in immodest bathing apparel, or passing through the streets to and from the beach without suitable covering, is prohibited at all times.

Bathing, fishing, and boating were prohibited on the Sabbath. Among the many other restrictions enforced on Sunday was the sale of all objects other than medicine. One druggist, who broke this law and sold a toothbrush to a visitor who had lost his, was forced to pay for his mistake with a fine.

What's more, there were curfew laws that required inhabitants of all dwellings to keep their shades up until 10 p.m., at which time the shades had to come down and all lights put out. Other curfew laws were aimed at young people. At certain times of the year no one under the age of 18 was allowed on the streets between 8 p.m. and daylight. Adding to the dismay of minors was an early law that prohibited dancing. As time went on the city fathers became a bit more open-minded, and a limited amount of social dancing was permitted. However, as late as 1920 an ordinance permitting dancing parties was issued with the following restrictions:

It is hereby declared to be unlawful for any person while dancing to assume or maintain any position which tends in any way to corrupt the good morals of any person attending said dance hall. Dances known as the tango, turkey-trot, bunny-hug, or shimmie, are hereby prohibited and declared to be unlawful.

Gambling of all kinds was forbidden, including games such as cards, dice, and billiards. Profanity was also prohibited, and all loud or boisterous talking and rude conduct was to be discontinued immediately, as it was not considered "in harmony with good order and propriety." As for liquor,

The buying, selling or giving away of any and all intoxicants, spirituous liquors, wine, beer, or cider, are strictly prohibited on any public or private property within one mile of the center of the original survey of the Retreat; and the Directors hereby request all well-disposed persons to promptly notify the Superintendent of any violations of this rule.

The sale of liquor within the city limits, as well as the establishment of bars or saloons, remained prohibited until 1969. For many years, Pacific Grove had the distinction of being the only dry town in California.

The preceding is only a partial listing of old Pacific

Grove's blue laws, but serves as proof of the Puritan tradition and regulated way of life there. The following note from a visitor in the late 1800s perhaps sums up the frustrations and feelings of many of the people.

Pacific Grove is a pretty but queer place. The Methodistical rules are stringent and the newcomers are kicking. Business places are not allowed in residence blocks. Boarding and lodging houses are not "business" but the butcher and baker are . . . One can roller skate there but not dance, can croquet but not billiard, while nary a card nor a euchre deck is tolerated. A quiet private nip is frequently taken, but no public drinking. While the laws are not so stringent as the famous blue laws of Connecticut . . . their effect is deadening to visitors. Among a few of the forbidden fruits are waltzing, playing the zither, reading the great Sunday dailies, selling popcorn on the beach, and playing ten pins.

Some of the Grove residents began to balk at the blue laws, as well as at a fence that encircled the area. Built during the retreat's early years, the fence began near the Chinese fishing village (near what is now the dividing line between the cities of Monterey and Pacific Grove) and extended around the entire community except for the waterfront. Among other reasons, the fence was erected to preserve the individuality of the area and to keep interlopers out. The stile mentioned by Robert Louis Stevenson provided access to the Grove for those on foot. Near the stile was a locked gate, which was the main entrance and exit for horse-drawn vehicles. The gate also kept "wagon merchants" out, so residents had to make a trip to the Grove's main entryway if they wished to purchase commodities from the peddlers who lined the Monterey side of the fence.

Another drawback to the gate, for residents as well as weekend visitors, was the bother of getting a key from the retreat office every time they wished to drive their wagons or carriages in or out of the enclosed area. This inconvenience is eloquently described by Lucy Neely McLane in her book A *Piney Paradise*. The gentleman she quotes is State Senator Benjamin J. Langford, who owned an imposing house near the waterfront and often visited the Grove on weekends. According to McLane's delightful book, the senator said:

Every time that I pulled up to the padlocked gate with my

Above: This Italian Villa-style house at 225 Central Avenue was built in 1884 by Senator Benjamin J. Langford, the man who "took an axe" to the retreat's gate. The house has long been a favorite of local history buffs. Photo by Chuck Scardina. Courtesy, Pacific Grove Tribune

Right: The Grove's first church building was this Episcopalian edifice known as St. Mary's-by-the-Sea, located on the southwest corner of Central Avenue and Twelfth Street. English Gothic in design, the church was modeled after a similar structure in Bath, England. Except for an extension of the sanctuary, the church remains much the way it was when it opened in 1887. Its beautiful interior includes signed Louis C. Tiffany stained glass windows and natural woods of pine, cedar, redwood, and walnut. Courtesy, Pat Hathaway Collection

family, I would have to dismount, go over the stile, hike about a mile to the Retreat office to get the key to unlock the gate, walk back to the gate, drive to the office to return the key in order that others might use it, unload my family and baggage, drive again to the office for the key, drive to the gate, unlock it, drive through, tie my horses, walk back again on foot to the office to leave the key; then, no matter how late the hour or how fatigued I felt, I would have to walk back to my carriage, drive to Monterey to be stabled, hire some equipage to return me to the fence, climb over the stile and limp to my house.

Langford effectively put an end to the era of Pacific Grove's locked gates. Approaching the fence one evening, he took an an axe from his carriage and, with a "senatorial swing," did away with the main gate. For all intents and purposes, this did away with all gate-related problems. After the gate was gone, the

In May of 1901 (only a few months before his assassination) President William McKinley visited the Monterey Peninsula, including Pacific Grove's flag-bedecked Methodist Church. In this photograph the presidential party is about to enter the twin-towered edifice. Completed in 1888, this imposing building was more to Pacific Grove than a church, serving as an assembly hall, a meeting place for Chatauqua gatherings, and the headquarters for several Methodist-related conferences. Due to "inadequacy and disrepair" the striking structure was torn down in 1964. Courtesy, Pat Hathaway Collection

Monterey land baron David Jacks was not only an important figure during the retreat's early days, but also the builder of these two houses. Built in 1881, the structures were located on the corner of Central Avenue and Fifteenth Street. Jacks is thought to be the man on the far left. Photo by C.W.J. Johnson. Courtesy, Pat Hathaway Collection

fence soon followed.

Soon the name of the retreat also changed. On July 16, 1889, the "kingdom by the sea" was incorporated as the City of Pacific Grove. Several other events of interest and importance took place during the 1880s, among them the building of two impressive and popular churches. Since Pacific Grove began as a Methodist retreat, one would expect a Methodist church to have been built first. Strange as it seems, it was the Episcopalians who erected the first formal church building. Organized within the confines of the retreat grounds in 1886, the energetic Episcopalians wasted little time in starting construction of their church. The striking structure was consecrated in July 1887. Modeled after the English Gothic design of a church in Bath, England, the Episcopal edifice became known as St. Mary's-by-the-Sea. In use to this day, the church is one of Pacific's Grove's most prized and cherished buildings. Not long after its completion, Miss Harriet Hammond of Chicago visited and fell in love with the picturesque structure. She canceled her

plans for a fashionable "windy city" wedding and arranged to be married at St. Mary's instead. The future Mrs. Cyrus H. McCormick and her husband-to-be, accompanied by approximately 40 friends and relatives in a private railroad car, returned to the Grove to be married in their adopted church.

As token of her thanks and as a memento of the occasion, the bride presented English embroidered white silk altar hangings to the church. Seven years later the happy couple returned to St. Mary's laden with gifts, including several large stained-glass windows, which can still be viewed near the entrance of the church. Many years later, after the death of his wife, McCormick commissioned the master craftsman Louis C. Tiffany to create a pair of floral glass windows for the church. Considered to be among Tiffany's finest works, the exquisite windows are treasured to this day by the congregation of St. Mary's; they add a touch of serenity to the Victorian interior of this beautiful sanctuary.

Following in the footsteps of the Episcopalians, the Methodists raised the twin towers of their church in 1888. Larger than St. Mary's and perhaps even more imposing, the Methodist Church was also used as an assembly hall and a meeting place for summer Chautauqua audiences, as well as church conferences. The impressive structure became "home" to the California Conference of the Methodist Church, which was held there for 31 years. This Pacific Grove landmark (which was unfortunately torn down in 1964) also boasted an impressive list of guests and lecturers, including President William McKinley in 1901.

Several other churches were eventually attracted by the seaside resort's religious climate. Over the years, Pacific Grove has often been called a "city of churches." Two other houses of worship constructed before the turn of the century were the Congregational Church (1892) and the First Christian Church of Pacific Grove (1895).

Another important nineteenth-century event was David Jacks' foreclosure on a portion of the property in the Grove. The Pacific Grove Retreat Association did not make the improvements that had originally been agreed upon and had difficulty making payments on the money Jacks had advanced. Jacks regained control of a portion of the property and proceeded to sell individual lots. Eventually he sold the entire package to the Pacific Improvement Company (discussed in the Monterey section of this book).

The Pacific Improvement Company agreed to honor the Retreat Association's goals and its deed restrictions. The community's success was ensured and important improvements began to be made.

Numerous new homes were built on a grand scale; some survive to this day as bed-and-breakfast inns. Also of importance was the construction of the impressive Hotel El Carmelo, which soon gained prominence as Pacific Grove's most elegant lodging house. Even though it was smaller in scale and not nearly as grand, its interior facilities were often compared to Monterey's Hotel Del Monte. Such comparisons were expected, since both hotels belonged to the Pacific Improvement Company. The *Del Monte Wave* newspaper wrote:

This October 1887 view looking south from near the entrance of the Hotel El Carmelo (later known as the Pacific Grove Hotel) shows a portion of the hotel's recently planted park-like grounds. Across Lighthouse Avenue one sees the block bounded by Fountain (left) and Grand avenues. The house facing Lighthouse Avenue, to the left of the Tuttle drugstore building and Ray's Hardware Store, is the home of J.O. Johnson, owner of the Mammoth Stable (the tower of which can be seen above Ray's Hardware Store). Photo by C.W.J. Johnson. Courtesy, Pat Hathaway Collection

Top: One of the Grove's most elegant lodging houses was the Pacific Grove Hotel, opened in 1887 as the Hotel El Carmelo. As the community of Carmel-by-the-Sea became better known, the establishment's name was changed to the Pacific Grove Hotel (and a Hotel Carmelo became a part of early Carmel). Like the Hotel Del Monte, it was owned and operated by the Pacific Improvement Company and thus became known as the "Del Monte" of the Grove. It featured elaborate gardens, an elevator of the "newest and most approved" design, superb cuisine and service, and views from all of its 114 rooms. The hotel was torn down in 1918. Courtesy, Pat Hathaway Collection

Above: It's Feast of Lanterns time again and Pacific Grove's Centrella Hotel is decorated appropriately. Originally known as the Centrella Cottage and later as the Centrella House, this hotel was constructed in the late 1880s. Today the building has been completely restored and welcomes guests as a bed and breakfast inn. It is located at 612 Central Avenue, across the street from the original Chatauqua Hall. Courtesy, Pat Hathaway Collection

To some considerable extent the interior of "El Carmelo" reminds one of its sister, the beautiful "Del Monte" . . . there is the same breeziness of lobby, the same inviting influence of drawing rooms, and the same general permission for enjoyment—and freedom from metropolitan restraint.

Opened in 1887, the commodious El Carmelo enjoyed many years of success. As the community of Carmel made its presence known, the hotel changed its name to the Pacific Grove Hotel and continued to function as "Queen of the Grove." In 1918 the hotel was torn down, and much of its lumber was used in the reconstruction of the Pebble Beach Lodge, which had burned in 1917.

A second guest facility of note is the Centrella Hotel, also constructed in the late 1880s. Today, approximately one century later, the Centrella has been restored to its original splendor and caters to visitors as a bed-and-breakfast inn. The Del Mar was another prominent Pacific Grove Hotel. Built in the 1890s, this handsome downtown structure was a part of Pacific Grove until 1953, when it was torn down to make room for a bank.

Boarding houses first opened in Pacific Grove in the 1880s. Among these Victorian structures was a building owned by J.F. Gosbey. It was rather plain in appearance upon its completion in 1887, but over the years the structure experienced many alterations and additions, and today is considered an excellent example of Queen Anne design. The building is now known as the Gosby House Inn. Like the Centrella,

Above: Another of the Grove's popular pre-1900 hotels was the Del Mar. Standing on the southwest corner of Lighthouse Avenue and Sixteenth Street, the bay-windowed building served visitors until 1953, when it was torn down to make room for a bank and parking lot. Courtesy, Pat Hathaway Collection

Left: Established in 1891, the Monterey and Pacific Grove Street Railway was a boon to the peninsula, and gained even more popularity in 1903 when the line was converted to electricity. In this photo a railway car stands in front of the Hotel El Carmelo on Lighthouse Avenue. Photo by C.K. Tuttle. Courtesy, Pat Hathaway Collection

it is a popular lodging house that caters to those who appreciate the charm of yesterday, with many of the conveniences of today.

In 1894, just to the west of the Gosbey House, Dr. A.J. Hart built a lovely house as his residence and office. Over the years this stylish structure (also of Queen Anne design) has become one of Pacific Grove's better known buildings, and has housed businesses of various kinds.

In addition to elegant lodging houses for people, a famous hotel for horses was built in 1884: the Mammoth Stable, owned by J.O. Johnson, one-time superintendent of the Pacific Improvement Company. For several years, passengers heading for the Grove disembarked from the train at the Monterey depot to

be welcomed by Johnson, who directed them to his coaches. Besides large carriages and well-kept coaches, Johnson also offered one-man buggies and speedy horses for those who desired fast transportation.

Johnson's Mammoth Stable more than lived up to its name. The structure boasted an elaborate tower that rose 80 feet in the air, as well as facilities for nearly 100 horses. In addition to rooms for harnesses, grain, and so on, the stable contained bedrooms, an office, a kitchen, and a dining room. Described as "one of the most extensive and complete stables in the state," and rated as "the largest, handsomest, most costly, and best equipped on the coast," Mammoth Stable became a great source of pride for Pacific Grove residents.

Above: Built in 1884 by J.O. Johnson, the Mammoth Stable straddled Grand Avenue and could house nearly 100 horses. It added considerable prestige to downtown Pacific Grove. Courtesy, Pat Hathaway Collection

Facing page, top: By 1907 development had come to Lover's Point. In this view one sees the beginnings of the Grove's permanent rock pier, a small observation house (the building to the right), and a Japanese Tea Garden (the oriental-style building to the left). Perhaps of most interest to early Lover's Point visitors were the glass-bottom boat rides, as advertised by the sign on the pier. The swan-bedecked boats (foreground) afforded dramatic views of the point's marine life and underwater gardens. Courtesy, Pat Hathaway Collection

Facing page, bottom: In this circa 1910 view from the Lover's Point promontory, the Del Monte Express steams along the Pacific Grove coast and heads for the nearby depot. The run from Monterey to Pacific Grove was one of the most scenic in the state. Courtesy, Pat Hathaway Collection

Another important means of transportation before the turn of the century was the Monterey and Pacific Grove Street Railway. Beginning in 1891, its brightly colored horse-drawn coaches were a great success. The run from Monterey's Hotel Del Monte to Pacific Grove's Methodist Church was described as "among the grandest scenic roads on the Pacific Coast." It is true that the original route—leading from the opulent Hotel Del Monte, through California's romantic first capital city, along the picturesque Monterey shoreline, and on into the pine-forested grounds of old Pacific Grove—passed many historic sites and provided its passengers with numerous scenic vistas. In 1893 the line became known as the Monterey and Pacific Grove Street Railway and Electric Power Company. The name change hinted at things to come, and the line was eventually converted to electricity. By 1903 the communities of Monterey and Pacific Grove boasted a modern link in the form of an electric streetcar line. Through the early 1900s the line remained a popular mode of transportation for visitors as well as residents. However, as the automobile became more and more commonplace, the Monterey and Pacific Grove streetcar was used less and less, except for a sharp increase during World War I. In 1923 the line closed down, and the tracks were torn up.

Other tracks that led from Monterey to Pacific Grove in the late 1800s were those of the Southern Pacific Railroad. The Grove continued to draw many

Above: These Pacific Grove ladies partake in tea and pleasantries at the Japanese Tea Garden on Lover's Point, circa 1900. Courtesy, Pat Hathaway Collection

Facing page, top: Faculty and students of the Hopkins Seaside Laboratory pose for a photograph during the summer of 1894. As the facility's reputation grew, it also outgrew its Lover's Point quarters, so in the early 1900s the station moved only a short distance away to Point Cabrillo, near the north end of Cannery Row where the Chinese fishing village once stood. The facility is now known as Hopkins Marine Station of Stanford University and has gained recognition and respect throughout the world. Photo by C.K. Tuttle. Courtesy, Pat Hathaway Collection

Facing page, bottom: An important part of the early Lover's Point scene were the buildings of Hopkins Seaside Laboratory. Established by Timothy Hopkins and funded by Stanford University, it was built in the early 1890s on land donated by the Pacific Improvement Company. The laboratory was the first marine station on the West Coast and offered research facilities for marine biologists, as well as programs for Stanford students and public school teachers who wished to increase their knowledge of marine life. The windmill to the right is thought to have pumped salt water to the facility. Also of interest is the wooden pier, which, for a time, graced the Lover's Point Beach. Photo by C.K. Tuttle. Courtesy, Pat Hathaway Collection

visitors from faraway places, and officials of the Pacific Improvement Company and Southern Pacific agreed that an extension of the Monterey line was in order. Pacific Grove became a busy transit point for trains to and from the peninsula. Even more scenic than the route of the Monterey and Pacific Grove streetcar line, the Southern Pacific tracks hugged the Pacific Grove shoreline and passed several picturesque promontories, including Lover's Point.

Some say that Lover's Point was known as Lovers of Jesus Point. Before that, it was Point Aulon (an old Spanish word for "abalone"). Over the years this area has been the site of several important functions, including prayer meetings. Just why the promontory became known as Lover's Point is open to question, but the writer of the following quote from an 1880 issue of the *Pacific Grove Review* had a definite opinion.

It is not only among the stately solemn pines where a friendly bush invites lovers to exchange confidences and plight their troth, but it is on the beach, where the discreet sea would no more reveal the stolen trysts along its boisterious margin than it would give up its dead, that one can see visions and hear sounds that should make the outgoing tide linger. If that rocky headland, known as Lover's Point, which projects its solitude away from the shore had only kept a day book of notes, or rather a night book of observations, how sensational would be its chronicles.

A rendezvous for lovers and a gathering place for prayer meetings, Lover's Point and its adjoining beach have also played other important roles in the history of Pacific Grove. The sheltered cove and white sands of "Main Beach" (Lover's Point Beach) have served for over a century as a favorite gathering spot for sunbathers and those who enjoy frolicking in the sea. In its early years the Lover's Point area, including its beach, pier, and bayside buildings, boasted such things as a Japanese Tea Garden, band concerts, a photo gallery, a bowling alley, "Feast of Lanterns" festivals, community bathhouses, a carousel, glass-bottom boat rides, a marine laboratory, an ice cream parlor, and a skating rink.

Among the most popular of these early attractions were the glass-bottom boat rides. Aboard these small vessels visitors and residents alike thrilled to the sight of the remarkable underwater gardens and marine life of the Lover's Point area. The Japanese Tea Garden,

housed in a building of oriental design, offered delicious cakes and teas served by ladies in traditional Japanese attire. However, the Hopkins Seaside Laboratory has perhaps evoked the most modern-day interest.

The marine laboratory was established by Timothy Hopkins in 1891. (Timothy Hopkins was the adopted son of Mark Hopkins, of San Francisco and Big Four railroad fame.) Inspired by Dr. Anton Dohrns' famous Zoological Station in Naples, Italy, Hopkins returned to America with dreams of a Stanford-operated marine research facility on the Pacific Coast. After presenting his plans to the proper authorities and consulting with selected Stanford professors, it was decided that Monterey Bay offered the type of environment and marine life they were seeking.

The Pacific Improvement Company donated land at Lover's Point. Enthusiastic help came from key Stanford personnel, including David Starr Jordan—noted ichthyologist and Stanford University's first president. A sizable two-story frame building was constructed, and the marine station got off to a very promising start. Soon a second building was added, and the Hopkins Seaside Laboratory began to gain international fame.

In the early 1900s it became apparent that the Lover's Point site was not big enough for the expanding station. A new location was found at Point Cabrillo, near the border of Monterey and Pacific Grove, site of the old Chinese fishing village. When the buildings there were constructed and put into use, the new facility became known as the Hopkins Marine Station of Stanford University.

The research laboratory has continued to expand. Today its neighbor is the Monterey Bay Aquarium (opened in 1984), and together these two unique

After the turn of the century, with "Bathhouse Smith" in charge, Pacific Grove's Lover's Point Beach took on a new look. Smith expanded the concession, increased the size of the beach area, added a boathouse, and greatly enlarged and improved the bathhouse. Nevertheless, the bathhouse eventually fell into disrepair, and was condemned by the city. Courtesy, Pat Hathaway Collection

house is located is admirably suited for the purpose, being well sheltered; but a new building with appointments for hot water is the ringing cry of the residents, that resounds and reverberates through the pine forest till all else is lost in that one appeal . . . When Pacific Grove can boast of good bathing facilities and suitable quarters to meet the demand, winter and summer, then she will "receive her share of the laurels that crown Monterey the Hotel Del Monte queen of watering places."

Through the 1880s and the 1890s, problems continued to plague the beachfront bathhouse, prompting additional comments from the *Del Monte Wave*:

Is it not about time that the miserable shell called a bathhouse . . . was replaced by one in which a person with the slightest degree of modesty might disrobe, without first stopping up numerous holes and cracks, to keep their next door neighbor from having a full view of the proceedings? The arrangement called by that name at present is a disgrace to the city, a disgrace to the owners and a standing opportunity for Peeping Toms.

By the turn of the century, the trials and tribulations of the bathhouse began to subside. William Smith acquired the waterfront facilities. With dynamite blasts, protested by various Pacific Grove residents, he proceeded to expand the beach. Smith also added a boathouse and enlarged and greatly improved the bathhouse. "Bathhouse Smith" (as he became known) has been credited with creating a bathing resort for the Grove.

In time Dr. Clarendon E. Foster took charge of the Lover's Point facilities and continued to operate the concessions well and respectably. Unfortunately, Dr. Foster eventually left the Grove to continue his medical practice in another California community.

After Dr. Foster's departure, the previous problems of the bathhouse again began to surface. Things came to a head when neglect and disrepair prompted the city to condemn the facility. The concession was now controlled by Mrs. Mattie McDougall, who also claimed much of the property adjacent to the bathhouse. Upon word of the city's action, she erected a barrier, preventing public access to the beach. But Julia B. Platt, not content to let McDougall control the popular beach, suggested to the city council that they

facilities add to our knowledge of life in the sea and help us to understand the mysteries of Monterey Bay.

Back at Lover's Point, another continuing and colorful attraction was the bathhouse. The first of a long line of such bathing facilities was built on Lover's Point in 1875. Unfortunately for salt-water bath buffs, the facility left much to be desired: it was described as "cramped, cold, and decidedly inadequate." As so often happened when Pacific Grove was in need, the Pacific Improvement Company came to the rescue. In the early 1880s the company built a new and improved bathing facility, featuring eight private salt-water baths. The residents of the Grove flocked to the waterfront to partake of the pleasures of their new bathhouse. As time went on problems again began to plague the facility. The importance of the bathhouse to the pioneer residents of the Grove is indicated by the following account from an 1884 issue of the *Del Monte Wave*:

Salt water baths are the one principal attraction at a seaside resort, and Sandy Cove Lover's Point Beach where the bath

tear the barrier down. The city fathers chose to play a waiting game, seeking a more amicable solution.

Citing the Grove's original deed, stating that "the Pacific Improvement Company guarantees public right of way to the beach," Platt decided that more decisive action was in order. She made her way to the locked gate and proceeded to file off the padlock. Platt was applauded by several of her Pacific Grove neighbors, who delighted in her boldness and chuckled at the sign she is said to have displayed:

Opened by Julia B. Platt. This entrance to the beach must be left open at all hours when the public might reasonably wish to pass through. I act in the matter because the council and police department of Pacific Grove are men and possibly somewhat timid.

McDougall countered with a second padlock, which Platt again filed off. Workmen then securely nailed the gate shut from the inside. Public use of the beach was at stake, and Platt again made her way to the board barrier, with a crowd on hand to witness the event. She set to work with an axe; in the tradition of Senator Langford, she dutifully did away with the barrier. Although a battle of words continued to be waged and legal ramifications were yet to be worked out, Julia B. Platt is credited with having put the McDougall matter to rest.

In this 1920s view, looking in a westerly direction from Grand Avenue, one sees the north side of Lighthouse Avenue. The buildings to the right (in the first block) still stand in the center of downtown Pacific Grove. The outlet with the extended awning was the B.F. Sowell and Son grocery store. To its right was the T.A. Work Co., a hardware outlet, and on the corner was the Bank of Pacific Grove. Across Forest Avenue was the Johnston Brothers store which specialized in drygoods. Further down the block was the E.B. Lewis Jewelry store. All the buildings in this block have since been demolished. In the next block, the building shown is still standing and at the time of this photograph was known as the Winston Hotel. The twin-towered structure in the background was the Methodist Church. The flag-bedecked streets and cars are thought to have been in observance of the Fourth of July. Courtesy, Pat Hathaway Collection

In addition to her antics with an axe (and the fact that she was to become Pacific Grove's first woman mayor), Julia B. Platt spent much of her time raking, hoeing, planting, watering, and, in general, beautifying the Lover's Point area. This remarkable lady also spearheaded a successful drive to remove the aged bathhouse and replace it with a swimming pool.

Local residents knew Julia Platt as a lady to be reckoned with, and a bit on the eccentric side. She was also an accomplished zoologist who held a doctorate degree from Germany's Freiburg University and had

Above: In 1924 Holman's Department Store opened on the block where the Pacific Grove Hotel once stood. The store is seen here from the corner of Lighthouse and Fountain avenues. During the Depression era a third story and a solarium were added, and the store gained fame as the largest department store between San Francisco and Los Angeles. Today the store is known as Ford's of Monterey Bay. Photo by D. Freeman. Courtesy, Pat Hathaway Collection

Below: Lodge Hall reveals architect Julia Morgan's distinctive blend of wood and stone, and the pleasing designs of the rustic original structures that are scattered about the Asilomar Conference Grounds. Seen here in 1934, the building today looks similar in most every way. Photo by Louis Josselyn. Courtesy, Pat Hathaway Collection

beach she fought to keep open and upon the picturesque promontory she loved so much.

Before she died, Julia Platt worked with a second well-known Pacific Grove resident, Wilford R. Holman, to arrange for a road that would make Pacific Grove more accessible to Carmel and other outlying areas. Their efforts were successful, and the road is officially known as W.R. Holman Highway, part of California's Highway 68.

W.R. Holman was the son of R.L. (Luther) Holman, who came to Pacific Grove in 1888. R.L. Holman and J.W. Towle operated "The Popular" dry goods store, which more than lived up to its name. But the cry of "Gold!" lured Towle from the Grove; he pulled up stakes and headed for the Klondike. The partnership was dissolved, and the store took the name of R.L. Holman.

Over the years the store continued to expand, moving to a succession of Pacific Grove locations. In 1905 Luther Holman turned over the operation of the store to his two sons, Wilford and Clarence, who rechristened it Holman's Department Store. In 1914 Wilford R. Holman became the full manager, and 10 years later he moved the store to a site it was to occupy (under the Holman name) for approximately 60 years. At this location—where the Pacific Grove Hotel once stood—a new two-story building was constructed. Holman's became known as the largest department store between Los Angeles and San Francisco.

The Depression years brought additional expansion to the store. However, some people felt that the large

served as a director of Italy's prestigious Naples Zoological Station. The talented Platt had a deep love for her adopted home town, and, according to historian Lucy Neely McLane, endeavored "almost single-handed" to make Pacific Grove a beautiful, progressive, and judiciously run city.

When she died in 1935, Pacific Grove lost a remarkable lady who was not afraid to fight for what she thought was right. Following her wishes, Julia B. Platt was buried at sea in a wicker basket. A gathering of city officials attended the ceremony on a boat. As the basket was slowly lowered into the sea, an airplane containing many of her friends circled the boat and dropped hundreds of roses upon the water. This grand lady is still remembered by those who know and love the history of the Grove. A marker in her honor has been placed at Lover's Point park, adjacent to the

establishment was out of character for the Grove and predicted a gloomy future for the energetic undertaking. Time proved the skeptics wrong; shopping at Holman's became a family tradition for residents of the Monterey Peninsula. In 1985 Holman's was purchased by the Ford's Department Store chain of nearby Watsonville. The store is now known as Ford's of Monterey Bay and continues to operate at the same location. Appropriately, the Ford name is well known in the Monterey Bay area; its Watsonville store is the oldest operation of its kind in California.

Members of the Holman family played other important parts in the community's development, bestowing many gifts on the people of the peninsula. Most recently the historic Holman house was donated to the Monterey Peninsula Museum of Art. Previously, they had given a collection of American Indian artifacts that are displayed in Monterey's historic, state-owned Pacific House. A collection of books about California donated by the Holmans is also housed in a state-owned facility, Pacific Grove's popular Asilomar Conference Grounds. It is most appropriate that these publications are housed at Asilomar, since this unique facility is used in part as a training center for employees of the California State Department of Parks and Recreation.

The Asilomar Conference Grounds are bordered on two sides by Pebble Beach and the Pacific Ocean, but the grounds are within the community of Pacific Grove. Beginning in 1913, when a YWCA group gathered there, this place of rolling sand dunes and picturesque pine trees has developed into one of the finest conference centers in the country. Asilomar's forest setting has been retained, and its natural wood and native stone buildings have been strategically placed within the contours of the land. The site has won praise by people from throughout the world as an example of human land use that respects the environment.

Julia Morgan, who is best remembered as the architect for the fabulous William Randolph Hearst Castle of San Simeon, California, developed the plans for the Asilomar grounds and its original structures. The Morgan-designed buildings form the nucleus of the conference center, but the overall grounds have grown to more than three times the size of the original 30-acre site (which was donated by the Pacific Improvement Company), and several additional

Built in 1889, the Holman house was one of Pacific Grove's early landmarks. Although the house still stands on the southeast corner of Lighthouse and Granite avenues, it is virtually unrecognizable. Its third story has been removed, a stucco exterior has been added, and parts of its roof have been hipped and covered with red tile. Standing to the left of the house is R. Luther Holman, the man who started the department store that was to take the Holman name. His son Wilford R. Holman, who developed the store into one of the most respected department stores in central California, is the lad sitting on the top step. After W.R. Holman's death in 1981, the house was given to the Monterey Peninsula Museum of Art. Courtesy, Pat Hathaway Collection

structures have been built. Following the pattern set by Morgan, the new buildings were designed to fit in with the sea, the sand, and the pines that surround them and have won several major architectural awards.

Today the Asilomar Conference Grounds are busier than ever and help to stimulate the local economy. The center handles an estimated 200,000 people per year and plays host to more than 1,000 organizations. Asilomar has truly become a refuge by the sea (as its name implies), and is a major drawing card for the visitor-oriented Monterey Peninsula.

Besides its popular conference grounds, its mild climate, and its rugged coastline, several attractions draw people to Pacific Grove. The community-oriented Good Old Days is an annual event that boasts antique cars, an arts and crafts fair, live entertainment, a colorful parade, pie-eating contests, a firefighter's competition, and a pancake breakfast. The most popular event of the fun-filled weekend is the Victorian Home Tour, in which residents open many Victorian homes to the public. People from throughout California and beyond flock to the Grove to view the carefully restored structures, beautiful both inside and out. A visit to these vintage buildings affords the opportunity to view old Pacific Grove and to appreciate the numerous architectural styles that help to make the community so appealing.

The Heritage Society of Pacific Grove can take much of the credit for renewing interest in the Grove's aged dwellings. It is a relatively young organization compared to Monterey's History and Art Association, but the Heritage Society has accomplished much in its short existence. It has established an "old-time" museum which complements the Grove's outstanding Museum of Natural History, and it co-sponsors the Victorian Home Tour in conjunction with the local Chamber of Commerce and the Pacific Grove Art Center. The Heritage Society researches and records all information pertaining to Pacific Grove's old buildings and awards a special "Heritage Plaque" to the owner of each such dwelling. These green plaques are displayed on many of the town's historic structures, making it possible to tell at a glance when the old houses were built and who the original owners were.

Also drawing visitors to Pacific Grove is another event that has evolved from the area's unique history: the annual Feast of Lanterns Festival. The festival began in 1905 and continues to be a popular summertime activity. According to tradition, the Methodist-sponsored Chautauqua movement at Lake Chautauqua, New York, closed its season with fireworks and a lantern parade along the shores of the lake. Since Pacific Grove was considered the Chautauqua of the West, it was only natural that it would stage a similar event in the summer.

Various sources describe the festival's origin in different ways. It is safe to say that the pageant was of Methodist origin, combined with Chinese overtones and interspersed with local touches. The original story involves Chinese villagers searching with lighted boats and hand-held lanterns for a Mandarin's daughter who has wandered off to drown herself rather than marry a nobleman chosen by her father. In the Pacific Grove pageant the search for the lovely

Chinese maiden is re-enacted year after year, but not because she is a potential suicide. She succeeds in fleeing with her lover, managing to elude the lantern-bearing searchers sent by her father. The pageant is staged in the evening on the colorfully decorated pier of Lover's Point Beach. The sandy beach and the walkways and rocks around it are crowded with spectators of all ages; some hold paper lanterns of their own, in keeping with the occasion.

Nowadays the festival has other attractions, including the crowning of the festival queen (who plays the part of the Mandarin's daughter) and her court. Over the years the festival has included such events as barbecues, sailboat races, tennis tournaments, golf tournaments (held on the city's beautiful 18-hole course by the ocean), band concerts, pet parades, fireworks displays, and lantern-bedecked boats that parade back and forth in the dark waters of the bay. Homes along the waterfront and throughout the town display brightly lit oriental lanterns in their windows and on their porches. No wonder Pacific Grove's Feast of Lanterns Festival is an eagerly anticipated event that continues to draw spectators from far and near.

Another Pacific Grove attraction is its park system. Visitors and residents enjoy strolling through these public places and picnicking in picturesque settings. Adjoining Lover's Point is the best known of all Pacific Grove parks. Situated along the rocky coast, between the scenic shore drive and the blue waters of the bay, is a stretch of land known as Perkins Park. Just as the dedicated work of Julia Platt was instrumental in the beautification of Lover's Point, the history of Perkins Park also revolves around a dedicated Pacific Grove resident. Hayes Perkins arrived in the Grove in 1938 and rented a cottage near the waterfront. He watched with dismay as young people playing along the shore caught poison oak. Perkins was immune to the poison, so he began pulling poison oak plants from the ground. He noted the ugly holes that were left and began beautifying the area by planting shrubs and ground cover that he had observed in his worldwide travels. One that he had seen in South Africa, named mesembryanthemum, was effective at smothering weeds, and also proved to adapt well to the Pacific Grove shore.

As his garden grew, the shoreline became a sea of color. People began to take note, and admirers from distant places journeyed to the Grove (usually be-

tween the months of April and August) to view "Perkins' posies." Hayes Perkins died in 1964, but his work has been continued by the city and by interested residents, and his "magic carpet" continues to grow. Among the tributes to this dedicated citizen and to his love affair with the Pacific Grove shoreline are pictures of his park that have appeared in more publications than there is room to mention. A 60-foot mural depicting Perkins' colorful garden of lavender and pink once graced the walls of New York's Grand Central Station.

Another of Pacific Grove's beautiful gardens can only be viewed from underwater: the Pacific Grove Marine Gardens. This marine wonderland has become a popular gathering place for scuba divers from throughout the West. Almost any weekend of the year, numerous diving enthusiasts can be seen enjoying the wonderful underwater plants and animals off the coast around Lover's Point.

Pacific Grove may be best known for the thousands of orange and black butterflies that fly around the town. During the months of October and November—since before man can remember— countless Monarch butterflies have found their way to the Grove. Traveling from as far away as the Rocky Mountains and perhaps beyond, these colorful creatures arrive every fall to make a small section of Pacific Grove their winter home. On warm sunny days during their stay, the Monarchs awaken and flutter about—a delightful sight. However, when the days turn cold and fog envelops the Grove, clusters of butterflies can be seen clinging to the branches and leaves of their chosen trees.

Celebrating the Monarchs' pilgrimage, Pacific Grove's schoolchildren honor the occasion with an annual parade. Dressed in colorful costumes, many featuring wings of orange and black, the children, along with their parents and throngs of local residents, celebrate the homecoming of the Monarchs. "Butterfly Town, U.S.A." gets caught up in this occasion as only a small town can.

More and more people are discovering Pacific Grove, and some residents look upon this with disfavor. They have chosen to live there because of the small-town atmosphere and the unique beauty of the area, and they fear that too many people and too much development will ruin both. But these very same qualities of Pacific Grove still prompt others to move there. It is hoped that those who are arriving now will remember what attracted them there in the first place. If so, they in turn will strive to keep their town as it started out to be: a peaceful paradise by the sea.

Mission San Carlos Borromeo del Rio Carmelo (Carmel Mission) was the hub of Alta California's mission chain. Father Junipero Serra founded this church in Monterey in 1770; however, due to a number of problems, the mission was moved to its present site in 1771. As the mission trail grew to 21 churches, Carmel Mission also continued to grow in size and importance. It was here that the leaders of the California missions lived, and it is here that two of the best-known padre presidents, Junipero Serra and Fermin Francisco de Lasuen, are buried. Carmel Mission's bell tower is seen here from the south; its bells still ring, reminding one of Carmel's unique link to the past. Courtesy, Harry Downie Collection

CHAPTER THREE

Carmel

PARADISE AMONG THE PINES

LIKE MONTEREY AND PACIFIC GROVE, Carmel boasts its own unique and colorful history. Located near the peninsula's south shore overlooking beautiful Carmel Bay, this quaint coastal community is known to people from throughout the world. Even though the Carmel of today is known for such things as its picturesque setting, lovely beach, unique architecture, famous personalities, and specialty shops, it will always be known to historians as the home of one of the most historic of all California missions.

Over two centuries ago, Father Junipero Serra—the leader of California's mission chain—founded the mission in old Monterey. The mission was moved to its Carmel site in 1771. The new location offered an abundance of fresh water and fertile land and was well removed from the troubles and temptations of Monterey. Padre Serra made his home there and introduced many local Indians to Christianity and the

Spanish way of life.

There are several versions of how the mission and the town came to be called Carmel. According to one theory, the explorer Sebastian Vizcaino named it when he sailed by in 1602 on the voyage in which he was to discover and name Monterey Bay. Passing the bay on the south side of the peninsula, he noticed a mountain that rose behind the bay and thought it similar to Mount Carmel in the Holy Land. Also desiring to honor a pair of Carmelite friars who were a part of his exploratory voyage, Vizcaino is said to have bestowed the name Carmelo on the mountain and the nearby valley.

A second version makes no mention of Mount Carmel, but does state that Vizcaino discovered a valley and named it for his patron saint, Our Lady of Carmel. Supposedly, the valley, the river, and the bay therefore came to be known by the name of Carmel. A third tale also mentions the fertile valley and simply states, "Sebastian Vizcaino in 1602 . . . permitted two Carmelite friars in his party to name El Carmelo in honor of their order."

The fourth version is similar to the first, in that it makes reference to the Holy Land's Mount Carmel. However, it credits Father Serra rather than Vizcaino with naming the area. As the story goes, after Serra decided to move his mission from Monterey, he noticed a mountain that looked like the biblical Mount Carmel. Near this mountain, in the vicinity of a fresh-water stream in the same valley that Vizcaino had seen, Serra chose to build his church. He blessed the area—including the valley, the river, and the mountain—with the name Carmelo. Because it was located there, the mission was also so named: Mission San Carlos Borromeo del Rio Carmelo.

Carmel Mission (as the old church is commonly called) prospered and became the hub of Alta California's Mission Trail. It also became the final resting place for its founding father, who is considered by some to be a saint in his own right. The name of Padre Junipero Serra will always be associated with Carmel and his beloved Mission San Carlos.

Because of events that took place at the mission, the Carmel area has been referred to as the literary capital of the western United States. This is because Father Francisco Palou spent time at Mission San Carlos during the 1770s and 1780s, during which he supposedly worked on "the first books written west

of the Alleghenies." The books Palou wrote were *Noticias de la Nueva California* (News of New California) and *Relacion Historica* (Historical Narrative), a biography of Serra. Of course, whether or not the spirit of Father Palou had anything to do with it, modern-day Carmel has a strong literary tradition, having attracted many authors and other creative artists.

During the heyday of the California missions, Mission San Carlos Borromeo del Rio Carmelo was the most prominent of all. The leaders of the early mission period lived there, and near the altar of its church two of the best known and successful "padre presidents" are buried. Unfortunately, after the secularization of the missions in 1833, the grand old church fell into disrepair. Eventually the property around the mission was acquired by a Scotsman who worked the land near the church and referred to his holdings as the Mission Ranch. A second Scotsman, Robert Louis Stevenson, visited the ruined mission during this period. In *The Old Pacific Capital*, he described the scene as follows:

The Carmel runs by many pleasant farms, a clear and shallow river, loved by wading kine; and at last, as it is falling towards a quicksand and the great Pacific, passes a ruined mission on a hill. From the mission church the eye embraces a great field of ocean, and the ear is filled with a continuous sound of distant breakers on the shore. But the day of the Jesuit [sic] has gone by, the day of the Yankee has succeeded, and there is no one left to care for the converted savage. The church is roofless and ruinous, sea-breezes and sea-fogs, and the alternation of the rain and sunshine, daily widening the breaches and casting the crockets from the wall. As an antiquity in this new land, a quaint specimen of missionary architecture, and a memorial of good deeds, it had a triple claim to preservation from all thinking people; but neglect and abuse have been its portion. There is no sign of American interference, save where a headboard has been torn from a grave to be a mark for pistol bullets. So it is with the Indians for whom it was erected. Their lands, I was told, are being yearly encroached upon by the neighbouring American proprietor, and with that exception no man troubles his head for the Indians of Carmel. Only one day in the year, the day before our Guy Fawkes, the padre drives over the hill from Monterey; the little sacristy, which is the only covered portion of the church, is filled with seats and decorated for the service;

the Indians troop together, their bright dresses contrasting with their dark and melancholy faces; and there, among a crowd of somewhat unsympathetic holiday-makers, you may hear God served with perhaps more touching circumstances than in any other temple under heaven.

If Robert Louis Stevenson had returned to the aged mission a scant five years after his 1879 visit, he would hardly have recognized the church on the hill. In 1882 Father Angelo Casanova of Monterey's Royal Presidio Chapel rediscovered the graves of Padre Presidents Junipero Serra and Fermin Francisco de Lasuen (as well as those of Fathers Juan Crespi and Julian Lopez), and started a movement to restore the most sacred of all California missions. Public interest was aroused and funds were raised. The restoration was accomplished and the church was rededicated in 1884, 100 years after Serra's death. Today Carmel Mission has the rank of basilica and is a registered National Historic Landmark.

Not long after Carmel Mission's restoration, Santiago J. Duckworth, an enterprising Monterey real estate agent, listened attentively to proposals of the Southern Pacific Railroad. These plans called for a branch-line from Monterey to Pacific Grove, and from there to the mouth of the Carmel River. The Methodist retreat of Pacific Grove was attracting people from far and near, and Duckworth envisioned a Catholic community near the peninsula's south shore, with the newly restored mission as its focal point. The railroad connection could help make this

Above: Secularization in 1833 brought disaster to California's missions. After the roof of Carmel Mission succumbed to the elements in 1852, the interior of this ancient church became a scene of ruin, as seen in this circa 1870s photo by C.W.J. Johnson. Courtesy, Pat Hathaway Collection

Left: In 1882 the bones of Father Junipero Serra were exhumed to prove that his earthly remains were still buried near the altar of the Carmel church. Father Angelo Casanova of the Monterey parish undertook the project to dispel rumors that Serra's remains had been dug up and distributed as relics. With this proof, public interest was aroused, and funds began pouring in for a mission rebuilding project to commemorate the 100th anniversary of Serra's death in 1784. Upon excavation of Serra's grave, the remains of Padre President Fermin Francisco de Lasuen, Father Juan Crespi, and Father Julian Lopez were also uncovered. Witnesses numbered approximately 400, including church dignitaries and uniformed members of San Francisco's St. Patrick's cadets. Father Casanova stands to the right of the graves, and caretaker Christiano Machado is seated at the center vault's edge. Photo by C.W.J. Johnson. Courtesy, Pat Hathaway Collection

Right: In this 1939 view, Harry Downie, John Yementes, and Father Michael O'Connell (l. to r.) pose for a photo during reconstruction of one of Carmel Mission's adobe walls. The 1930s were important years for the mission; during this period Downie was placed in charge of removing the 1884 peaked roof and restoring the mission to its original 1797 appearance. A cabinetmaker by trade and an acknowledged authority on California missions and the life of Father Serra, Downie devoted nearly 50 years of his life to mission restoration work, primarily at Carmel. Photo by Louis Josselyn. Courtesy, Pat Hathaway Collection

Below: Father Angelo Casanova's 1884 mission restoration project left the church with a peaked roof, which was not in keeping with the building's original design. Although this may have upset historians of the time, Casanova's goal was to preserve the structure and make the church usable, and in this he succeeded. The peaked roof, seen here in the late 1880s, remained in place until the mid-1930s, when Harry Downie restored the roof to its original appearance. Courtesy, Pat Hathaway Collection

In the late 1880s, and into the early 1890s, Carmel was little more than a dream. Santiago J. Duckworth advertised it as "Carmel City," a proposed "Catholic Summer Resort." In his dreams Duckworth saw his "city" as a rival to Pacific Grove's popular Methodist Retreat. During this time some development took place, and a hotel catered to visitors who found their way to the peninsula's south bay. A portion of the hotel can be seen in this 1890s view looking east toward "upper" Ocean Avenue, the current main entrance into Carmel. Photo by C.W.J. Johnson. Courtesy, Pat Hathaway Collection

idea a success.

Duckworth and his brother worked out an agreement with Honore Escolle (owner of the land that contains much of present-day Carmel) for the development of approximately 325 acres of prime property. S.J. Duckworth began advertising the proposed development of "Carmel City" in 1889. The advertisement stated that the object of the promoters was to build a Catholic summer resort.

Unfortunately for the Duckworth brothers and their proposed community, plans for the Carmel River railroad were derailed somewhere along the way. Undaunted, S.J. Duckworth continued to promote the Catholic community, and a number of lots were sold. Soon a few houses were built among the pines, and a small hotel catered to visitors. Improvements were made, and new partnerships were formed. Abbie Jane Hunter (founder and president of the San Francisco-based Women's Real Estate Investment Company) took an active part in the proceedings. However, the Carmel City development did not progress as rapidly as hoped, and before the turn of the century the Duckworth brothers abandoned their venture.

Even so, the publicity helped establish the Carmel area as more than the home of the historic Mission

San Carlos. The *Salinas Weekly Register* reported as follows:

Carmel City now has a good hotel and a number of neat cottages, some of which are owned by San Francisco parties, who propose to summer at that delightful resort. The Pacific Improvement Co.'s water pipes are laid above the town and furnish an abundance of pure water. The soil is good and the climate so mild and genial that residents are embowering their homes with flowers. After a visit to the place one does not wonder at the number of real estate transactions that have been had in reference to the property at that point.

Above: The Hotel Carmel, established around the turn of the century, was located on the northeast corner of Carmel's main intersection, Ocean Avenue and San Carlos Street. After a fire destroyed part of this heavily-shingled building in 1931, the remaining portion was torn down. Standing near the building's main entrance are Dr. and Mrs. A.A. Canfield, who operated the hotel at the time this photograph was taken circa 1908. As evidenced in the picture, this central Carmel location also served as a stage stop. Sightseeing coaches, as well as stages that operated on the Monterey-Carmel run, left from this point. Courtesy, Pat Hathaway Collection

Right: This small building is said to be Carmel's first frame house. Seen in 1919, it remains a part of old Carmel. Over the years there have been many alterations and additions, and the historic structure is difficult to recognize as the quaint cabin appearing in this photograph. Photo by Louis Josselyn. Courtesy, Pat Hathaway Collection

The *Pacific Grove Review* also had flattering things to say about the development on the other side of the peninsula. "The beautiful little city with the finest view in the world is rapidly building up. Purchases are daily being made . . . lovely homes are being built."

Local publicity was all well and good, but much more important was an enthusiastic description of the beauty of the area that appeared in a pre-1890 issue of the prestigious *Scribner's Magazine*. The U.S. government surveyor who wrote the report was David Starr Jordan (introduced in the Pacific Grove section of this book.) So impressed was Jordan with the peninsula's south shore that many years later, serving as president of Stanford, he purchased property from the Carmel Development Company and started a trend that brought numerous professors from the University of California and Stanford to the area. It was not long before a section known as "Faculty Row" sprang up near the waterfront, adding a touch of class to the seaside settlement.

In the early 1900s there were new rumors that a railroad was coming to town, and the future of the Carmel area again looked bright. However, the railroad again failed to arrive, and Carmel's growth became slow and measured. Frank H. Powers and James Franklin Devendorf, founders of the Carmel Development Company, continued to acquire property in the Carmel area, and before long they owned much of what was to become Carmel-by-the-Sea. This name, by which the community is officially known, first appeared in print prior to the turn of the century and is attributed by some to Abbie Jane Hunter's Women's Real Estate Investment Company.

As the years went by, more property was acquired, the treeless tracts were cleared and planted, and much of the land was subdivided. However, there was no great desire to build a major metropolis, so the mood of Carmel remained tranquil and the community continued to be regarded as a peaceful village. Among those who found delight in the area's solitude, and inspiration in its beauty, were writers, painters, and other people of the arts. They shared their happiness and their homes with others of their kind, and the community's developers encouraged more of them to settle on its shores.

Among the earliest of the "creative folk" to discover the charms of Carmel's woods, sand, and sea were poet

Carmel's co-founder Frank Devendorf poses for this circa 1916 photograph depicting four generations. Seated in front of Devendorf is his mother, Grace Aram; sitting on her lap is Devendorf's grandchild, Elizabeth Gibbs; and on the right is one of Devendorf's four daughters, Myrtle Devendorf Gibbs. Devendorf donated land for the park that bears his name, situated near the center of the Carmel business district. Photo by Louis Josselyn. Courtesy, Pat Hathaway Collection

George Sterling and novelist Mary Austin. Not long after their arrival the San Francisco earthquake and fire drove other literary people out of the Bay Area. The idyllic life of Carmel attracted them, and the beautiful village soon received an influx of settlers. Joining the writers in their trek to Carmel were artists and musicians. Soon the area became known for attracting people of an unconventional sort.

With authors and artists leading the parade, the colony of Carmel continued to grow. The village became noted for camaraderie and companionship. For example, members of the community rallied around Herbert (Bert) Heron and helped make a

Above: On Sunday afternoons, poet George Sterling often gave abalone parties on Carmel beach. From the rocks, he would venture into the water and seek the rock-clinging shellfish. Sterling was among the first of the "creative folk" to discover Carmel, and his influence brought several other authors to the area. This photo by E.A. Cohen was taken on May 16, 1908. Courtesy, Pat Hathaway Collection

Right: One of Carmel's oldest and best-known hotels is the Pine Inn. Even though it had its beginning around the turn of the century, and boasts more than 75 years of continuous service, this aged edifice is perhaps even more popular today than it was in its early years. The original Hotel Carmelo literally became a part of the Pine Inn establishment in 1903, when it was put on rollers and moved down Ocean Avenue to the Pine Inn site. Today it is a part of the main hotel structure and continues to be a haven for visitors to Carmel-by-the-Sea. Photo by L.S. Slevin. Courtesy, Pat Hathaway Collection

success of his Forest Theater, the first of the state's outdoor community theaters. Much of the town took part, and audiences and critics came from as far away as San Francisco and Los Angeles. The plays were performed with considerable acclaim, and many local playwrights experienced the thrill of seeing their works performed in their own town, on a stage among the pines and under the stars.

One peninsula publication of the past suggests that Jack London wrote a Forest Theater production, *The First Poet*, in 1915. It is true that London visited Carmel in its early years and enjoyed outings and evenings with his writer friends there. However, recent research has cast doubt on his Forest Theater involvement. Evidence indicates that it was written instead by his good friend George Sterling.

Mary Austin, writing in 1927, described the idyllic life of Carmel's early authors and artists:

We achieved, all of us who flocked there within the ensuing two or three years, especially after the fire of 1906 had made San Francisco uninhabitable to the creative worker, a settled habit of morning work . . . But by the early afternoon one and another of the painter and writer folk could be seen sauntering by piney trails . . . there would be tea beside driftwood fires, or mussel roasts by moonlight—or the lot of us would pound abalone for chowder . . . And talk, ambrosial, unquotable talk . . .

Of course, many residents of old Carmel were not part of this group and in the beginning many disapproved of the creative people's social activities. But as time went on the villagers got to know one another, and a community spirit began to prevail. Soon the various groups were appreciated for what they were, and it was discovered that the authors and artists were not such a bad lot.

During this early period property was cheap, and living was even cheaper. Friends shared what little they had, and many of the villagers asked only to be left alone so they could pursue their craft. The small community continued to grow in size, and a handful of stores were established. Besides the hotel, which was eventually moved and became part of Carmel's popular Pine Inn, there was a bakery, a stationery store, a butcher shop (open on a twice-a-week basis), a drugstore, a barber shop, a dry-goods store, a plumbing shop, a hardware store, a candy shop, a restaurant, and a general merchandise store.

Another important facility in the village was the Carnegie Coastal Laboratory, a branch of the Department of Botanical Research of the famed Carnegie Institution of Washington, D.C. A group of leading botanists and research scientists began to arrive in 1910. These men of science and the professors of Faculty Row found much to discuss during afternoon walks and evening talks.

The arrival of new businesses and people and the continued development of Carmel began to change the town. No longer was it an isolated place in which to paint and write; changes were coming, and something had to be done. In 1916 a meeting was called and Carmel was incorporated as a city. A flurry of laws were enacted. Fortunately, the new rules were written by farsighted officials who respected their town and what it stood for. They did everything in their power to preserve the coziness and character of their village.

Among the laws that helped Carmel retain its charm was a ban on the cutting of trees, which is strictly enforced to this day. Not a single limb of a city-owned tree may be cut unless the City Forestry Commission (on its monthly "tree tour") views the tree in question and approves the cutting. Permission must also be obtained to remove any tree that is on private property within the city limits. Over the years, its multitude of trees has helped make Carmel the unique community that it is. Situated in a forest setting with a profusion

In the early 1900s one of Carmel's annual events was the Dutch Fair sponsored by the Arts and Crafts Club. This popular activity was full of surprises and attracted people from far and near. Perhaps the biggest surprise of the 1909 Fair was the pipe-smoking "woman" of rather large size (left), who just happened to be the future Nobel Prize-winning author Sinclair Lewis. Lewis acted as barker and master of ceremonies for the food and flower booths. Photo by L.S. Slevin. Courtesy, Pat Hathaway Collection

of trees lining its narrow streets—and in many cases growing in the center of them—Carmel has become known for its woodsy atmosphere. Residents jealously watch over and protect each of the town's estimated 35,000 trees.

Several other ordinances have helped Carmel perpetuate its village atmosphere. A zoning ordinance passed in 1929 stated that business development should forever be subordinate to the residential character of the community. This law helped Carmel keep its beach free of commercial development, restricted the construction of high buildings, prohibited electric signs, and discouraged the installation of street lights and sidewalks in the residential areas.

Carmel is known for the many things it has, such as its beautiful scenery and picturesque setting, but it

Above: Other than imaginative entryways, many houses within the Carmel city limits have names instead of numbers. When a guest has lost his way, a familiar sign can save the day. Photo by R.A. Reinstedt. Courtesy, R.A. Reinstedt Collection

Below: At the intersection of Ocean Avenue and San Carlos Street stands Carmel's World War I Memorial Arch. This scene shows the dedication ceremony for the November 11, 1921, laying of the monument's cornerstone. The memorial honors the 56 Carmel men who left the village to fight in the First World War. Photo by Louis Josselyn. Courtesy, Pat Hathaway Collection

is also known for the many things it does not have. There are no house numbers, so residents often place imaginative signs and names on the dwellings. Since there is no home mail delivery, residents must visit the post office for their mail. There are no schools within the boundaries of Carmel-by-the-Sea (admittedly a very small area). However, the Carmel Unified School District encompasses an area slightly less than half the size of the state of Rhode Island. Among other things that Carmel doesn't have are parking meters, traffic lights, supermarkets, cabaret entertainment, jukeboxes, billboards, courthouses, and jails. The absence of such items have helped Carmel to retain its charm and small-town feeling.

Many cultural events, colorful activities, and famous personalities have been associated with the town. The name Carmel was connected with the arts very early, and over the years numerous authors and artists have lived in the area: Lincoln Steffens, Mary DeNeale Morgan, Upton Sinclair, Ferdinand Burgdorff, Sinclair Lewis, Sydney Yard, Harry Leon Wilson, Richard Partington, Jesse Lynch Williams, Chris Jorgensen, James Hopper, Jo Mora, Ray Stannard Baker, Laura Maxwell, Fred Bechdolt, William Chase, Van Wyck Brooks, William Watts, Talbert Johnson, William P. Silva, Sam Blythe,

Three of Carmel's early writers were (left to right) Fred Bechdolt, James Hopper, and Michael Williams. This talented trio produced many short stories published in such well-known magazines as The Saturday Evening Post, Colliers, and Harper's Weekly. Bechdolt and Hopper collaborated on the popular novel 9009, which provided an impetus for much-needed prison reform. Photo by L.S. Slevin. Courtesy, Pat Hathaway Collection

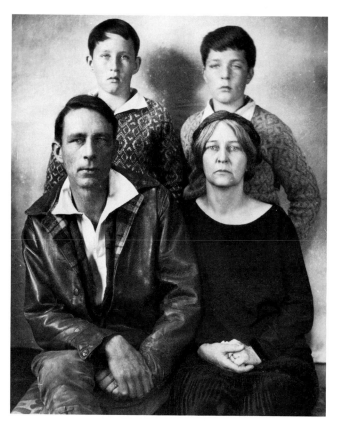

Above: Robinson and Una Jeffers pose with their sons Garth and Donnan in this February 10, 1929, photograph by Louis Josselyn. Jeffers lived in Carmel from 1914 until his death in 1962. Courtesy, Pat Hathaway Collection

Right: Certainly among the most respected and best known of Carmel authors was the poet and playwright Robinson Jeffers. Jeffers and his wife, Una, first came to Carmel in 1914. At the first opportunity they purchased a five-acre site near Carmel Point, and on this beautiful Carmel Bay shore they built Tor House. Tor is roughly defined as a "rocky hill," and it was upon their own private "tor" that their house was built. As the house was being constructed of granite from the nearby beach, Jeffers worked along with the stonemasons and soon mastered the craft. Proof of his mastery is the fabled Hawk Tower (right) which he created single-handedly as a tribute to his wife, as well as a place of solitude and a spot to write. Tor House proper was completed in 1919, and Hawk Tower (named after a hawk that frequented the tower when it was being built) was finished in 1924. Today these historic stone structures are a part of the National Trust for Historic Preservation. Photo by Louis Josselyn. Courtesy, Pat Hathaway Collection

Henriette Shore, Michael Williams, and Irene Alexander, to name but a few. Of course a name that has become synonymous with Carmel and the nearby Big Sur coast is that of the famed poet Robinson Jeffers.

Additionally, many famed photographers have been associated with the area. Two internationally known giants in the world of photography are Ansel Adams and Edward Weston. Adams was a relative newcomer, having lived in the area from 1962 until his death in 1984. Both he and Weston made their homes in the community of Carmel Highlands, slightly to the south. A few of the other noted photographers who have called the Carmel area home are Arnold Genthe, Emile Bruggiere, Louis Slevin, Johann Hagemeyer, Louis Josselyn, George Seideneck, Wynn Bullock, and Steve Crouch.

Carmel of old was also the home of numerous musicians and performers. Such people naturally sought outlets for their talents, and the 1920s and 1930s are often called the golden years of Carmel culture in this respect. This period witnessed the beginning of many music and drama organizations, including the Carmel Music Society, founded in 1927.

This organization, the Monterey Peninsula Orchestra Association, and Dene Denny and Hazel Watrous of the Denny-Watrous Gallery, were instrumental in starting the Carmel Bach Festival. Since its inception in 1935 this annual festival has become famous for showcasing the music of Johann Sebastian Bach. It now lasts three weeks and attracts acclaimed participants and spectators from many lands. Numerous other music activities have taken place in Carmel, including the founding of the Monterey County Symphony in 1946.

Drama has also played an important part in the history of Carmel. After the Forest Theater, a second theater opened its doors—and a new era for local thespians—in 1924. The Golden Bough took drama more seriously than the Forest Theater and catered to those who were more concerned with the fine art of acting. In its new building, which was described as "the most nearly perfect playhouse of our day," a school of dramatic arts was also established. Succeeding in its efforts to bring serious theater to Carmel, the Golden Bough was said to have ushered "a new era in the development of drama into California." With Edward G. (Ted) Kuster at its helm, the Golden

Top: With music and history blending within this beautiful church, a Bach Festival performance at Carmel Mission is an experience one will not soon forget. Courtesy, Carmel Bach Festival

Above: Sandor Salgo has been music director and conductor of the Carmel Bach Festival since 1956. During these years the festival has grown from a small, one-week event to an internationally acclaimed, 21-day festival. The recipient of numerous awards and a guest conductor of famed orchestras in many lands, Maestro Salgo has become as much a Carmel tradition as the festival itself. Courtesy, Carmel Bach Festival

Another stone house near Carmel Point, and not far from Jeffers' Tor House, was in its early days the home of Edward G. (Ted) Kuster. Kuster is remembered by Carmelites for a variety of things, including his efforts to bring serious theater to Carmel, and for his development of the Golden Bough Theater. The beautiful home still stands near the intersection of Bay View and Inspiration avenues, but is rather difficult to see because trees and houses partially surround it. Photo by Louis Josselyn. Courtesy, Pat Hathaway Collection

Bough enjoyed considerable success. However, as time went on Kuster spent much of his time traveling and leased the theater to various individuals and organizations. During this period the theater had its ups and downs. In 1935, after a performance of *By Candlelight*, fire gutted the Golden Bough. Not one to give up, Kuster opened a second Golden Bough in a different Carmel location, alternating between screenings of foreign films and live performances. In 1949 the second Golden Bough was also destroyed by fire. By coincidence, the second fire also followed a performance of *By Candlelight*. Today a third Golden Bough stands on the site of the second structure, and one can't help but wonder if *By Candlelight* will ever appear on its marquee.

Early Carmelites also enjoyed a number of sporting and recreational events. Foremost among these was an annual softball series. These Sunday afternoon "Abalone League" contests were favorites with a great number of the villagers. The league has the distinction of being the first such organization in the western United States. The first field was on the Carmel Point promontory, a location that played an important part in the naming of the league. According to old-timers, a home run usually went over the Carmel Point cliffs into the water and rocks of the bay. Among these rocks lurked a variety of creatures, including a type of sea mollusk known as abalone. A combination of home runs, lost softballs, and tasty creatures from the sea supposedly gave the league its name. Of course, the naming of the league may also have been a whimsical reference to the popularity of abalone at the parties of the Carmel cultural set. So popular was this shellfish that a song was written about it, and its praises were sung in a variety of imaginative and earthy verses at many long-ago gatherings.

Old-time Carmelites also enjoyed a variety of beach-oriented activities. A beach house was built near the west end of Ocean Avenue (Carmel's main street) and became a popular gathering place. It served several purposes, including provision of all the necessary equipment for "surf bathing." Other popular recreational activities in the early years included hiking, horseback riding, and playing golf on a 10-hole golf course that stretched from Carmel Point to the mouth of the nearby Carmel River.

Among the recreational events long associated with the village are the Carmel Kite Festival and the Carmel

Built in the late 1800s, Carmel's beach house at the west end of Ocean Avenue featured a glass-enclosed pavilion that was a popular gathering place for people of all ages. College girls often worked at the facility during the summer, and for 25 cents one could rent a bathing suit, a towel, and have use of a shower and dressing room. The redwood board-and-batten structure was often used for parties by clubs and organizations. The glass-enclosed section is seen here on September 13, 1905. Photo by E.A. Cohen. Courtesy, Pat Hathaway Collection

Above: The Bloomin Basement building is a good example of quaint Carmel architecture. Following a trend started by designer and builder Hugh Comstock, Carmel has become known for its unique homes and business buildings. The architecture adds to Carmel's charm and attracts countless people to the area. Photo by Louis Josselyn. Courtesy, Pat Hathaway Collection

Below: Living up to its name, Carmel's Great Castle Contest features elaborate castles in the sand. Photo by R.A. Reinstedt. Courtesy, R.A. Reinstedt Collection

Mission Fiesta. Another local favorite is the Great Sand Castle Contest, which dates back to 1962. It has become so popular the organizers now try to limit the size of the crowds and to keep it a local event. The sponsoring organization, the Monterey Bay Chapter of the American Institute of Architects, refuses to announce the date of the contest until a few days before it takes place. Even so, the word spreads fast, and people from far and near make their way to the beach with an assortment of digging tools and picnic baskets in hand.

It is not only the fanciful designs of the sand castles that draw people to Carmel, but also the architecture of its unique dwellings. Many of the early residents lived in cottages and cabins of rather diminutive size, a surprising number of which exist to this day. These buildings of "board and batten" construction, with their crooked lines and peculiar designs, formed the basis for "Carmel style" structures that were to follow. Many of these early dwellings now have cement foundations, modern heating systems to complement their original fireplaces, inside plumbing, and an array of towers, turrets, and gingerbread trim.

Board-and-batten cottages predominated in the beginning, except for a few more elaborate structures on Faculty Row and elsewhere. But Carmel is probably best known for its buildings of a "Mother Goose" design, inspired by Hugh W. Comstock, who arrived in Carmel in 1924 to visit his sister. He met

a pretty local lass by the name of Mayotta Brown, who soon became his bride. The new Mrs. Comstock was talented in a variety of fields, especially in making dolls. Buyers came from far and near to purchase her products of rag and felt, and soon every nook and cranny of the Comstock home was filled with her colorful creations. The newlyweds decided to build a "doll house" in the woods, where the dolls could be shown in a setting all their own. Hugh Comstock possessed artistic talent as well as a variety of building skills. With the able assistance of his wife, he set to work designing and building a "people-sized" doll house. The fairytale cottage became the talk of the town, and Carmelites besieged Comstock to build them doll houses of their own. The idea soon caught on with village merchants, and Comstock kept busy designing and building the fanciful structures. When he completed the popular Tuck Box Tea Room building in 1926, Carmel's *Pine Cone* newspaper described Hugh Comstock as the village's "builder of dreams."

Carmel has had many other such builders over the years, talented architects who lent their names to many of Carmel's homes. Hugh Comstock himself graduated from Mother Goose designs to structures of other kinds, and in his later years he was widely known

The Tuck Box, perhaps the best-known structure within the city limits of Carmel-by-the-Sea, was designed and built by Hugh Comstock. Upon its completion in 1926, Comstock was described as a "builder of dreams," and for many a chance to come to Carmel and live in a Comstock cottage of "Mother Goose" design was certainly a dream come true. Even though the building was known as Sally's when this photograph was taken, it became the Tuck Box Tea Room more than 50 years ago, and remains as such to this day. The Tuck Box is located on the east side of Dolores Street, between Ocean and Seventh avenues. Photo by Louis Josselyn. Courtesy, Pat Hathaway Collection

for his work with "Post Adobe" construction. Even though Carmel today boasts a variety of exotic and imaginative architectural styles, when people think of the village they most often think of fairytale cottages nestled in the trees. In this way they pay tribute to Hugh and Mayotta Comstock, the creators of Carmel's people-sized doll houses among the pines.

Outsiders also think of Carmel as a picturesque village on a beautiful bay, a weekend hideaway where shopping is a treat and enjoyable dining is easy to find. Even though it is small in size, its attractions loom large to those who seek an unusual vacation retreat.

The area of the city is only one square mile, and

In addition to its scenic setting, unique dwellings, and sought-after shops, Carmel also boasts one of the best-known mayors in America. Actor/director Clint Eastwood overwhelmed his opposition and was elected mayor on April 8, 1986. After the publicity died down, most Carmelites agreed that Eastwood not only was an able administrator, but also had a deep love for his village by the sea. Photo by Holly McFarland. Courtesy, Carmel Pine Cone

the population is less than 5,000 people. However, this tiny seaside settlement has enough fine shops, galleries, and restaurants to please the most discriminating visitor. As for accommodations, Carmel boasts many delightful inns within the downtown area, and a surprising number of guest houses can be found in nearby neighborhoods.

Amidst all of this hustle and bustle, Carmel has somehow succeeded in remaining small in feeling, as well as size. Even though more than 1,000 business licenses have been issued, the village has retained a definite degree of individuality. Part of this can be attributed to its setting and to its strict building codes. Almost everything—except visitors—is limited in size, shape, and number. The most important factor over the years has been Carmel's people, whose desire to maintain the charm of their town has kept it manageable. Perhaps the biggest things about the Carmel area today are the number of annual visitors who flock to its shores and the prices of the homes that overlook

its beautiful beach.

Beginning with people like Powers and Devendorf, many individuals have worked to preserve the character of Carmel. It may seem unfair to single out one person who represents what Carmel was meant to be, but there is an individual who stands out from the rest. Perry Newberry, during his 28-year stay in his adopted home town, served his community in many ways, including as editor of the *Pine Cone* newspaper and mayor (chairman of the board of trustees). He was known as a champion of the "no growth" cause and fought against progress, commercialism, paved streets, numbers on houses, destruction of trees, home mail delivery, regimented architecture, street lights on the corners, millionaires' mansions, and businesses on the beach. Newberry spearheaded many of Carmel's strict zoning laws. He was an accomplished artist even before coming to Carmel; his enthusiastic involvement helped make many of the village's theatrical productions a success; and the children's stories he wrote are still remembered and read. Newberry participated in practically every other phase of early Carmel life, including the nightly gatherings of writers and wits who frequented the village's favorite watering spots. It has been said that if Powers and Devendorf were the fathers of the village, Perry Newberry most certainly must be considered its foster father.

The strong feelings that so many have for Carmel are reflected in the words of a former resident who often returned to reminisce with friends and enjoy the atmosphere. During one of these visits, he remarked to a reporter:

Somehow, strangely enough, Carmel has survived and retained much of the atmosphere that made it famous in the days when I first lived here. For God's sake, don't let the Babbitts ruin the town. You've got every other city in the country beat.

The man who spoke these words was Sinclair Lewis, the first American writer to win the Nobel Prize for literature. Babbitt, the title character in one of his novels, can be characterized as "an uncultivated businessman." Even though a few "Babbitts" have managed to sneak in, Carmel, in the eyes of many people, still "has every other city in the country beat."

Above: Monterey's Fisherman's Wharf boasts markets, restaurants, and shops that attract visitors throughout the year. Photo © 1987 Bill Paullus

Left: Boats line the Monterey marina. In the background, the Doubletree Inn stands to the right, and in the center is the Hotel San Carlos, where the Monterey Sheraton is now located. Photo © 1987 George Elich

Previous page: The sardine may be gone, but Monterey's Fisherman's Wharf is still a center for sport-fishing boats, as well as one of the most picturesque wharves on the California coast. Photo © 1987 Jerry Lebeck

Until 1964 the Witch Tree stood on Pescadero Point.
Before a Pacific storm blew down this aged Monterey
Cypress, it was a popular attraction on the Seventeen
Mile Drive. It got its name because some saw the shape
of a witch's head in the tree. Photo © 1987 Lee Blaisdell

Left: The Monterey Bay Aquarium's kelp forest grows in a tank 29 feet high and open to the sky, the tallest such exhibit in the nation. Courtesy, Monterey Bay Aquarium

Below: Looking south toward the Monterey Bay Aquarium at dusk, one sees its distinctive rooflines and architecture that reflect those of the Hovden Cannery, which once stood on the site. Courtesy, Monterey Bay Aquarium

Above: During the months of October and November countless Monarch butterflies descend on a small section of Pacific Grove to make their winter home. On warm days the Monarchs flutter about; when it turns cold, they cling to the leaves and branches of their chosen trees, as seen in this circa 1960 photo. Photo © 1987 Lee Blaisdell

Right: This fairytale cottage in the forest started Carmel's trend toward buildings of a "Mother Goose" design. Built by Hugh Comstock and his wife in the mid-1920s, the home is known to old-time Carmelites as the "doll house." Photo © 1987 Jerry Lebeck

Left: Carmel Beach, seen here circa 1960, is a favorite place for surfers, sunbathers, and sand castle builders. Residents and visitors often gather here to watch the sun set on the Pacific. Photo © 1987 Lee Blaisdell

Below: On the south side of Carmel Point lies Carmel River State Beach. Not as well known as Carmel Beach, it attracts many locals who enjoy the sun and surf. Photo © 1987 Roger Fremier

Of all the trees and countless sights of the Pebble Beach area, the Lone Cypress is the best known. Described as "one of the world's most photographed trees," this Monterey Cypress is not only symbolic of Pebble Beach, but of the Montery Peninsula as well. Photo © 1987 Orville Andrews

CHAPTER FOUR

Pebble Beach

A MAGNIFICENT MEETING OF LAND AND SEA

PEBBLE BEACH IS THE AREA SURROUNDED by the Pacific Ocean and the communities of Carmel, Pacific Grove, and Monterey. It is also referred to as the Del Monte Forest or simply "the Forest." This area is often described as the most beautiful part of the Monterey Peninsula.

Much of what is now Pebble Beach was once part of the Mexican land grants Punta de Pinos (Point of Pines) and El Pescadero (Fishing Place). About 1840 El Pescadero, the largest of the two grants, was owned by Doña Maria del Carmen Barreto, the widow of Fabian Barreto, who had acquired the land in 1836. She was unhappy with ranch life and yearned instead for the social whirl of California's capital city. Doña Maria wanted a "good adobe casa in Monterey where . . . a woman could look out on life and romance," so she sold the beautiful Rancho Pescadero for $500 and bought a house in the nearby capital.

Above: From the very early days, tolls were charged at the entrances to the Del Monte Forest-Pebble Beach areas. This gate was located atop Carmel hill. The toll in 1914 was 25 cents for a vehicle containing three people or less. Photo by L.S. Slevin. Courtesy, Pat Hathaway Collection

Below: When this 1901 photo was taken, the gate house at the Pacific Grove entrance to the Seventeen Mile Drive boasted a sign reading "Forest Lodge." At this time, the gate was located at the head of Forest Avenue. Here we see the caretaker, who also doubled as the toll collector, and his son. Photo by L.S. Slevin. Courtesy, Pat Hathaway Collection

The more than 4,000 acres that Doña Maria sold is now some of the most sought after real estate on the California coast, and $500 won't even pay for an overnight stay in the Vizcaino suite of the Lodge at Pebble Beach.

Until the turn of the present century, when Monterey, Pacific Grove, and Carmel were growing and developing separate personalities, the Pebble Beach area continued to slumber. However, changes had taken place at the Pescadero site. David Jacks had bought the property, and in 1879 he sold it to the Big Four railroad barons. Their Pacific Improvement Company built the Hotel Del Monte in Monterey and opened the Pebble Beach side of the peninsula by developing the Seventeen Mile Drive, a famous attraction for guests of the hotel. The farthest reaches of the scenic tour lay in what is now Pebble Beach.

The magnificent meeting of land and sea drew people to the area, as did the beauty of its wooded trails and Monterey Cypress trees. These trees are native to the peninsula and nearby Point Lobos. Among the many cypress trees that cling tenaciously to the rugged headlands along the Seventeen Mile Drive shore is one that has become symbolic of the entire Monterey Peninsula. Majestic in its solitude on an outcropping of stone, the tree seems to dare Pacific winds and ocean storms to sweep it from its perch. This tree has become known as the Lone Cypress and is one of the world's most photographed trees. Robert Louis Stevenson described the hauntingly beautiful cypress trees as "ghosts fleeing before the wind." They show odd shapes and twisted lines from years of

In this pre-1900 view, a family of four pauses for the photographer amid a grove of cypress trees along the Seventeen Mile Drive. Courtesy, Pat Hathaway Collection

Above: In the Pebble Beach area's early days a Chinese fishing camp was located on what is now known as Stillwater Cove. Stories of smuggling opium, sake, and people from across the sea were associated with the camp. Among its inhabitants was the Sun Choy family, seen here circa 1890. Courtesy, Pat Hathaway Collection

Facing page, top: A picnic in the Del Monte Forest was a favorite pastime for early peninsula residents and visitors to the Pebble Beach area. This outing took place in 1896. Courtesy, Pat Hathaway Collection

Facing page, bottom: A short walk from the Chinese fishing camp at Stillwater Cove was the pebbly beach from which the area gained its name. The beach, seen here in the 1890s, was a favorite stop for Hotel Del Monte guests and Seventeen Mile Drive enthusiasts. If one were to stand at this site today and look in the same direction, one would see the famed 18th fairway of the Pebble Beach Golf Links. Courtesy, Pat Hathaway Collection

resisting tormenting winds. These survivors remain as much an attraction today as they did when the Seventeen Mile Drive first beckoned to visitors to explore this side of the peninsula.

Early travelers who accepted this invitation were thrilled by the scenes they saw. One such treasure was a secluded inlet on El Pescadero's south coast, known today as Stillwater Cove. This protected cove had a colorful history. A Chinese fishing camp had been located there, and besides the catching of fish and drying of seaweed, other activities are said to have been associated with the settlement, including the smuggling of opium, sake, and people from across the sea. It remained a mystery where the human cargo was bound, but it was suspected that the opium and sake found their way to the Chinese village on the peninsula's opposite shore.

Also on the shores of this sheltered cove was a beach that became a favorite of Hotel Del Monte guests. Many of the visitors aboard the hotel's horse-drawn tallyhos would stop there for a picnic and a refreshing romp in the surf. The beach became known for its Carmel Bay vistas and for the thousands of shiny

In 1915 Samuel Finley Brown Morse became manager of the Pacific Improvement Company properties. Rejecting plans that included developing small lots on the Pebble Beach shore, Morse hired his friend Jack Neville to design a championship golf course nestled among the trees atop the headlands overlooking Carmel Bay. The Pebble Beach Golf Links and its new, prestigious lodge were completed in 1919. In that same year Morse formed the Del Monte Properties Company and purchased the Monterey Peninsula holdings of the Pacific Improvement Company. Under Morse's leadership the Del Monte Properties Company would develop the Pebble Beach area while preserving its unique beauty. Morse is seen in a 1924 photo by Julian P. Graham. Courtesy, Pat Hathaway Collection

pebbles that were washed ashore by the sea. The area was so sought out as a "pebble picking place" that in 1908 a lodge of logs was built near the shore. The lodge and the areas adjacent to it became increasingly popular, and with the help of a golf course built nearby, the vicinity has gained international fame as Pebble Beach.

The man responsible for developing the Pebble Beach Golf Links was Samuel Finley Brown Morse, a graduate of Yale University and grandnephew of Samuel Finley Breese Morse, the inventor of the telegraph. The Morse influence wasn't felt until the mid-teens, but he spent considerable time prior to that visiting the Hotel Del Monte and its fabulous grounds and became impressed with the area's beauty. In 1915 Morse became manager of the Pacific Improvement Company properties. This was an event of great importance to the Monterey Peninsula; it marked the beginning of Pebble Beach as we know it today.

Morse was displeased with the plans that were in progress when he arrived, which included development of small lots on the Pebble Beach shore. He envisioned "the forest left intact," with a championship golf course nestled among the trees atop the headlands overlooking Carmel Bay. His good friend Jack Neville, who was widely known for his golfing exploits, eagerly accepted the job of designing the Pebble Beach links. With the help of other noted golfers, Neville laid out a course that is respected by enthusiasts in every land and is considered one of the most challenging and beautiful in the world. During construction of the Pebble Beach links, the popular lodge of logs was destroyed by fire. Since this establishment was an important part of his overall plans, Morse designed a new lodge of more elegance and prestige. The lodge and the golf course were both completed in 1919.

In the same year Morse formed the Del Monte Properties Company and purchased the Monterey Peninsula holdings of the Pacific Improvement Company, including the Hotel Del Monte. With Morse leading the way, Pebble Beach was awakened from its slumber by a plan that would develop the area while preserving its unique beauty. Rather than homes by the hundreds and miles of concrete, Morse felt that greenery, golf courses, and other recreational facilities would be best for Pebble Beach. The Monterey Peninsula Country Club and the exclusive Cypress

Point Golf Club soon added their courses to this golfer's paradise. All three of the Pebble Beach courses feature fairways in the forest and holes bordering the sea; they became known for their difficulty of play, especially when ocean breezes blew, as well as for their beauty.

The Monterey Peninsula Country Club added a second 18-hole course to its grounds in 1963, and the Spyglass Hill golf links opened for play in 1966. Many major golfing events are now held on the Pebble Beach courses. The Pebble Beach, Cypress Point, and Spyglass Hill links host the popular AT&T Pebble Beach National Pro-Am Tournament. This event was founded by the late Bing Crosby and is referred to as "the Crosby" or "the clambake" by many golf enthusiasts. The first and most traditional of such tournaments, it draws tens of thousands of visitors to the Monterey Peninsula each winter. Golf promises to remain very much a part of the Pebble Beach way of life; the beautiful Poppy Hills Golf Course opened in 1986, and the Spanish Bay links and resort complex are due to open in the fall of 1987.

Other recreational and sporting events have helped to put Pebble Beach on the map. Among the most popular of these attractions were the Pebble Beach Road Races of 1950 to 1956, which became known as the classic of America's sports car road races. This event played an important part in reviving road racing in the United States, but the races attracted too many people to the tree-lined circuit. The overcrowding, the increased speed of the automobiles, and the many

Top: Because of the Pebble Beach area's beauty and the popularity of Stillwater Cove, a lodge of logs was built near its sheltered shore. Completed in 1908, the lodge became a favorite "stopping off place" for those who toured the Seventeen Mile Drive. The lodge was destroyed by fire during the construction of the Pebble Beach Golf Links. Courtesy, Pat Hathaway Collection

Above: Not long after the lodge of logs was destroyed by fire, S.F.B. Morse started work on a new lodge of more elegance and prestige. Opened in 1919, along with the Pebble Beach links, the lodge and golf course soon became popular among the sporting set. In this photograph, thought to have been taken in the late 1920s, one gets a look at the "new" Del Monte Lodge (now known as the Lodge at Pebble Beach) and its immediate environs, including the famed 18th green of the Pebble Beach Golf Links. Courtesy, Pat Hathaway Collection

Above: The unique Macomber mansion was of rustic design and boasted rooms that were massive in size. Upon its completion in 1917, Mr. and Mrs. A. Kingsley Macomber moved into their country estate, gave an elaborate dress ball, and then left the retreat, never to return. The Monterey Pine mansion sat vacant for more than 40 years, except for a caretaker who watched over the grounds. During the 1960s the aged lodge of logs was occupied once more, and this photo is thought to have been taken during that time. By 1970 the house was vacant again, and serious vandalizing occurred. On April 28, 1977, a fire destroyed the Macomber home. Today little remains of this estate except memories and stories of strange happenings that are said to have taken place. Courtesy, Pebble Beach Company

Facing page: From patios, porches, and picturesque front yards, the Pebble Beach mansions situated along the shore boasted beautiful vistas of the rugged Pebble Beach coast. Courtesy, Pebble Beach Company

dangers involved prompted the building of the Laguna Seca race track east of Monterey in 1957. The mood is different, but Laguna Seca has gained an envied reputation all its own and continues to attract visitors to the peninsula.

A holdover from the exciting days of road racing in the forest is the prestigious Pebble Beach Concours d'Elegance, which showcases rare and exotic automobiles once a year. This elegant event, which celebrated its silver anniversary in 1975, is considered by many to be in a class by itself. People and cars from all over the world take part. Entrants find the jewel-like setting on the lawn of the Lodge at Pebble Beach, overlooking the 18th green of the Pebble Beach links and the beautiful blue waters of Carmel Bay, to be without equal.

Equestrian sport has played a significant role in the history of Pebble Beach recreational activities. By the 1920s, there were more than 100 miles of bridle paths in the forest. Today the Pebble Beach Equestrian Center is known as the most complete riding establishment on the West Coast. Among the popular events that take place there are the Pebble Beach Summer Horse Show and the Pebble Beach Dressage Championships. Polo is also played in Pebble Beach.

Another animal-oriented activity is the annual Del Monte Kennel Club Dog Show. Like the Concours d'Elegance, this event is held on the lawn of the Lodge at Pebble Beach. Entries are limited to "champions only," but the show draws hundreds of entrants from throughout the nation; to win at "Pebble" is the ultimate dream of many participants.

Other social and recreational activities revolve around the private Beach and Tennis Club, which has catered to countless famous personalities over the years and continues to play an important part in the lives of many peninsula families. A recreational outlet for the wealthy set was a house near the lodge. Known to old-timers as Canary Cottage, the yellow building still stands and boasts a beautiful view as well as a remarkable past. One of the area's earliest homes, it once harbored a casino "of sorts." Only the "right" people, holding invitations and dressed in appropriate attire, were allowed inside. This miniature Monte Carlo offered its guests exciting games such as craps and roulette. The "right" people, of course, were the ones who could afford to lose. Those who didn't fit into that category were welcome to stay, but advised not to play.

Another dwelling of early Pebble Beach was a most impressive sight. Of gigantic proportions, and made entirely of Monterey Pine logs, the mansion was located on a country estate that overlooked Carmel Bay and covered an area of more than 75 acres. Its immense dining room, shaped like a cube, measured 30 feet in length, 30 feet in width, and stretched to an amazing 30 feet in height! All the rooms had similar king-size dimensions. The living room, which doubled as a ballroom, was as big as many homes: 1,800 square feet. The fireplace in the main room, which was one of four in the house, was built of native stone; its opening was 8 feet high and 12 feet wide.

The history of this stately place is among the most interesting of any Pebble Beach estate. The grandiose retreat was constructed in 1917 for A. Kingsley Macomber, a millionaire friend of S.F.B. Morse. Macomber and his wife (a Standard Oil heiress and wealthy in her own right) moved into their cavernous log cabin, gave an elaborate dress ball, and then left the retreat—never to return. For more than 40 years the massive Macomber mansion sat vacant. Vandals occasionally made a call; it is said that a foray during Prohibition relieved the wine cellar of its vintage French wines. A caretaker watched over the grounds and assorted ghosts who were said to frequent the place.

During much of the 1960s the Macomber house was occupied once more. However, by 1970 the rustic retreat was vacant again. Innocent trespassing then gave way to serious vandalism, and the grand old building was soon in sad need of repair. In 1977 a fire destroyed the once luxurious lodge, leaving only memories and mighty stone spires.

Many palaces of early Pebble Beach remain, elegant edifices sprinkled about the forest and perched on rocky bluffs. These dwellings were once occupied by people of fashion and fame, who came to Pebble Beach before the Depression put an end to their extravagant lifestyles. They built magical mansions with castle-like designs, featuring pillars of marble, pools on the beach, eye-catching turrets, priceless antiques, travertine towers, fixtures of gold, prized works of art, and, perhaps most cherished of all, magnificent vistas of the Pacific and the distant mountain peaks.

Things have changed; people of more modest means are now able to share in the Pebble Beach dream. To be sure, it is still home to people of wealth and fame, but its mystique also belongs to others who have become a part of Pebble Beach. Whether one lives there or not doesn't really matter; all who visit this special place have S.F.B. Morse to thank for his foresight and his love of the land. Without this man of vision, there would undoubtedly be shopping malls, urban sprawl, and buildings on the beach. Instead, there are golf courses, greenbelts, and vistas beyond compare, surrounded by elegance and a forest of picturesque trees. Thanks to S.F.B. Morse, "the Duke of Del Monte," Pebble Beach remains one of the most beautiful places in the world.

In this 1927 photograph, members of the Carmel Volunteer Fire Department and the community's lone traffic officer pose in front of the fire department's prized LuVerne fire truck. Photo by Louis Josselyn. Courtesy, Pat Hathaway Collection

CHAPTER FIVE

Partners in Progress

While the economy of the Monterey Peninsula is nowadays dependent on the military and tourism, it is the ocean itself, the shimmering waves of the Monterey Bay, that created industry and brought population to the area. If you asked the typical peninsulan to name a product of business that is historically associated with Monterey, the answer would be "sardines" or "canneries." We still fish the bay for calamari and other delicacies, but the business of hosting visitors to our shores far exceeds that of luring fish to our nets.

People come here to enjoy one of the world's most beautiful coastlines, and even the military originally encamped here because of the navy's use of the port. Commodore John Drake Sloat of the U.S. Navy claimed the area for the Union in 1846, ending the rule of Mexico.

To go back a bit further, all the way to 1602 when the Spanish explorer Vizcaino "discovered" Monterey, he found the place thickly populated with native Americans—who, of course, were accomplished fishermen.

In 1770 the Spanish returned to the bay, led by Father Junipero Serra, who founded the Carmel Mission and other missions along the coast. Sea otter pelts were the booming business of the day, once again showing that mankind draws a living from the sea. These cute little fellows are now protected by federal law, however. We don't kill them for their fur, but photograph them for our scrapbooks.

Pirates arrived in port in the early 1800s, and in 1822

Mexico captured Monterey from Spain. The United States then attacked the Mexicans—by sea, naturally—in 1842 and 1846. The original capital of California, Monterey hosted the state's first theater and first newspaper, called the *Californian.* Government business joined whaling as important industries of the mid-nineteenth century here.

It was only a matter of time before Monterey would realize its potential as a resort town by the sea, and that time came in 1880 with construction of the elegant Hotel Del Monte. It was simply the grandest hotel west of the Mississippi, and visitors came from around the world to stay there. The Hotel Del Monte had 500 rooms and cost one million dollars to build at a time when such a sum was nothing short of staggering. A poster of the day described it as "The Paradise of the Pacific, Where It is Always Summertime."

If you've ever endured a February storm on the Monterey Peninsula, you might tend to doubt the veracity of that claim. But today you can see the Monterey Aquarium, the Pebble Beach community, the happy throngs at Lover's Point Beach in Pacific Grove, and realize that the ocean continues to be the area's greatest asset.

The companies whose stories follow have chosen to support this important literary and civic project. They illustrate the many ways individuals and businesses have contributed to the growth and development of the Monterey Peninsula.

MONTEREY HISTORY AND ART ASSOCIATION

The Monterey History and Art Association was founded in 1931 as a nonprofit corporation for the purpose of preserving Monterey's historic heritage and, in particular, the old adobe homes and other historic buildings of early Spanish, Mexican, and American California.

Monterey has more historic adobes than any other city in California, thanks to the efforts of the association and its dedicated membership. "It is beyond contradiction that every important historical event in California from 1770 to 1848 began or ended in Monterey, and that the buildings associated with these events are the greatest of Monterey's tangible assets," wrote Colonel Roger S. Fitch, the first president and a founder of the association. The historical structures that have been preserved are still very much in use as offices, homes, and public museums.

Among the association's historic buildings: Casa Serrano, 412 Pacific Street, saved from being turned into a parking lot in 1959 and now the

association's headquarters; Fremont Adobe, 539 Hartnell Street, now leased for business purposes; Francis Doud House, 177 Van Buren Street, an early American wooden house, surrounded by the Carmel Martin Memorial Garden; and the Mayo Hayes O'Donnell Library, formerly the first Protestant Church in Monterey, now housing an outstanding collection of Californiana.

The Joseph Boston Store, located in Casa del Oro at Scott and Olivier streets, first opened for business during the Gold Rush in 1849 and has been reopened to sell items representative of its early days. The building is owned by the State of California, while the store and the adjacent herb garden are operated and maintained by the association.

The Allen Knight Maritime Museum portrays the old sailing ship era, the fishing and whaling days in Monterey, and the local naval history that is so important to the nation and to California. The museum, established in 1970, is sponsored by the association and has filled its small quarters on Calle Principal with a comprehensive collection of nautical

Casa Serrano exterior from a drawing by Olaf Dahlstrand.

artifacts—from the time Commodore John Drake Sloat landed and took possession of Monterey and California in 1846 through the sardine era of Cannery Row. So great is this maritime collection now, that plans are under way to build a new Maritime Museum on Custom House Plaza.

The association continues to take an active role in informing both the residents and visitors to the Monterey Peninsula of the inestimable value of Monterey's heritage through a series of ongoing programs and special events: the annual Adobe Tour on the last Saturday in April, the historic site signs on the Path of History that guide visitors through Old Monterey, the commemoration of Commodore Sloat's landing with ceremonies the first week in July at the Sloat Monument and the Custom House Plaza; and the historic costume workshop in Pacific House with an additional display in a portion of Doud House. Through the courtesy of association volunteers, the Casa Amesti, a National Trust for Historic Preservation property, is open to the public on weekends.

Each June on the first Saturday the Monterey History and Art Association's membership and honored guests celebrate Monterey's birthday and pay tribute to the many volunteers and supporters that help preserve the heritage of Monterey.

The cake-cutting ceremony at the Merienda celebrating Monterey's birthday.

MONTEREY FEDERAL CREDIT UNION

American Banker magazine released the results of its third consecutive annual national consumer survey in late 1986 which showed that again people who used credit unions were significantly more satisfied with their financial institution than were customers of banks and savings and loans. Credit union members cited more personal, friendlier service, a common bond in a nonprofit membership organization, and greater ease in procuring a loan as reasons for their preference. Monterey Federal Credit Union certainly benefits from that kind of loyal support; from its humble beginnings in 1968, MFCU has grown to 25,000 members with assets in excess of $70 million and is one of the fastest-growing and most successful credit unions in the nation. Today people who live or work in Carmel, Monterey, Pacific Grove, Pebble Beach, Del Rey Oaks, Sand City, or Seaside enjoy the "common bond" that allows them to join together. But it wasn't always so.

The credit union opened its doors on October 23, 1968, in the basement of Hermann Hall at the Naval Postgraduate School—but only during the lunch hour. Membership was limited to NPS personnel and employees, yet the infant enterprise took in deposits of nearly one million dollars in the first 10 weeks. The need was clearly there, as by 1970 the credit union had a full-time manager, full-time hours, and served 2,400 members.

The first break into wider public service came in 1974, when the charter was rewritten to open the credit union to the entire population of the city of Monterey. The newly christened Monterey Peninsula Federal Credit Union, with assets of five million dollars and 5,000 members, merged with the Carpenters' Local Credit Union, and opened the main office at 550 El Estero, facing the picturesque El Estero Lake, home of ducks, geese, and colorful paddleboats, in 1975.

For the next five years the com-

munity flocked to its credit union. Computers were added, checking accounts first offered in 1976, and the Sand Dollar was adopted as a corporate symbol and as a name of the member newsletter. But the charter expansion of 1980, to include six new communities on the Peninsula, was the major thrust that has made MFCU a national leader and phenomenal triumph as a true community credit union.

In December 1980, after opening its spacious new offices at 2600 Garden Road, the credit union had assets of

Credit union founders and officials took part in the charter signing ceremony on October 23, 1968, which established the forerunner of today's Monterey Federal Credit Union.

$17 million with 13,600 members. In 1981 the Seaside Credit Union merged into Monterey Federal and assets grew to $20 million with 15,000 members. In 1982 the Pacific Grove office at 161 Fountain Avenue was opened, helping the credit union to record growth with loans up 35 percent and savings up 42 percent from the previous year. The National Association of Federal Credit Unions, recognizing the credit union's extraordinary popularity and innovative marketing, honored Monterey Federal as Credit Union of the Year in 1983.

By the mid-1980s MFCU had embarked on a five-year plan aimed at the goals of $113 million in assets and 30,000 members by 1990, realistic goals as Monterey Federal members continue to enjoy the superior service and rate advantages unmatched by

other financial institutions. As of now, the consumer can find virtually every banking service at any of Monterey Federal's five conveniently located offices.

MFCU's checking accounts feature not only minimal service charges, but also pay interest with no minimum balance. Loan rates on automobiles, mobile homes, and boats have been historically lower than bank rates, and now the credit union's real estate loans on first trust deeds have been expanded to a maximum 30-year term. Both money markets and IRA accounts pay higher interest than offered by the banks, and fully 15 percent of MFCU's loans are unsecured "character" loans to its members. MFCU loans money only to its members, so that all of its funds are put to use in the community.

Automatic Teller Machine (ATM) "Exchange" cards have been issued so members can use them to gain more convenient access to their cash nationwide. Monterey Federal also offers credit cards and "VOCAB," which provides members computer access to their various accounts via touch-tone phone. The electronic age may have arrived, but those who prefer to do their banking on a person-to-person basis will still find the friendliest service at MFCU. The Monterey office located at Franklin and Figueroa and the Pacific Grove branch are even open Saturday mornings, and the credit union is the kind of place where customer and staff know one another and enjoy the chance to exchange casual, as well as business, information.

Monterey Federal Credit Union truly belongs to its members, the communities it serves, and really takes care of them. Despite exponential growth, it hasn't lost that personal touch, that dedication and commitment to the people of the Monterey Peninsula. The community continues to give Monterey Federal an overwhelming vote of confidence and support.

HIGHLANDS INN

The Highlands Inn, when it was constructed in 1916, served as an exclusive country club and meeting center for the residents of lush Carmel Highlands, south of Carmel on Coast Route 1 to Big Sur. The palatial main lodge, with its twin granite fireplaces and mesmerizing views of Point Lobos and Yankee Point, was the community's center, and the adjacent cabins were used to accommodate guests of Highlands families. The lodge's classical elegance is said to have influenced the famous architect Charles Greene, who built the stone James House, which the inn overlooks, in 1918.

Novelist Daniel James and his wife, Lilith, remember the early years of the Highlands Inn. Through the 1920s and 1930s the inn gained considerable popularity among artists and writers, including poet Robinson Jeffers and adventure author Jack London. The Jameses brought John Steinbeck and Charlie Chaplin, among others, to the Highlands Inn. It was long a favorite rendezvous of Hollywood's most glamorous stars and the perfect spot for elegant weddings and romantic honeymoons.

The rich history of the Highlands Inn has served it well. While Clark Gable and Myrna Loy are no longer with us, on a recent stay you might have spotted actress Kim Novak, composer

Every guest room at the inn commands a breathtaking ocean view.

Marvin Hamlisch, actor James Whitmore, or actress/model Brooke Shields dining at the inn's Pacific's Edge restaurant or shopping at its gourmet California Market. World-renowned photographer Ansel Adams was a great friend of the Highlands Inn.

But the inn today, after a three-year renovation that has won top honors from professional architecture and interior design organizations, scarcely resembles its former self. One hundred and three brand-new units have replaced the small cottages, which were in disrepair when new ownership took over in 1982, and 43 rooms were extensively remodeled. The main lodge, which had been furnished in heavy Victorian style with red velvet-covered sofas and plaid carpeting, has been opened up with dormer windows and skylights to make a large, airy room that takes advantage of one of the world's most dazzling ocean views.

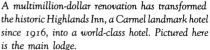

A multimillion-dollar renovation has transformed the historic Highlands Inn, a Carmel landmark hotel since 1916, into a world-class hotel. Pictured here is the main lodge.

Indeed, every one of the guest rooms, now furnished in a California contemporary style, enjoys a spectacular view of the sea. Most of the units also include a six-jet spa bath with full ocean outlook and a fireplace well-stocked with wood. Monterey architect Will Shaw designed a grand stairway to the lodge entrance, and the dining rooms and lounges have all been redesigned to lighten the atmosphere and focus attention on the 180-degree panorama, which includes excellent whale watching in season.

"Repetition of sleek geometric shapes and the absence of extraneous details convey an Art Deco feel that is simultaneously sophisticated and low-key," the *San Francisco Chronicle* enthused. The new Highlands Inn has received top honors from both the American Society of Interior Designers and the Monterey Bay chapter of the American Institute of Architects. Amenities include three outdoor hot tubs, a swimming pool, and California cuisine in both the Pacific's Edge restaurant and the California Market deli and tavern.

The Highlands Inn has come a long way since 1916. Following its multimillion-dollar refurbishment, it is now restored to its original luster and grandeur; it is once again the jewel of the central coast.

NATIONAL PRO-AM YOUTH FUND

The National Pro-Am Youth Fund is the successor to the Bing Crosby Youth Fund founded by the late crooner and golfer and funded by his annual golf tournament at Pebble Beach. Like the event itself, the Youth Fund dropped the Crosby name in 1986, when AT&T took over sponsorship of the Monterey Peninsula's premier sporting event. By whatever name, however, the Youth Fund has been helping good causes for 30 years, and is one of the largest benefactors in Northern California. In 1987 the fund will distribute a half-million dollars to youth groups, cultural organizations, and the handicapped.

Bing Crosby brought his golf tournament here from Rancho Santa Fe near San Diego in 1947, and the Youth Fund was chartered in 1957. From 1959 to 1962 the fund itself conducted the tournament. Since 1962 it's been managed by volunteers (chief among whom was Crosby himself) with the fund existing as a separate entity that receives all the proceeds and distributes them in the community. Eighty percent of the fund's grants are given to organizations on the Monterey Peninsula, with an additional 10 percent distributed in Salinas, Santa Cruz, and other parts of Northern California.

"Thanks to the great success of the tournament, and now to AT&T's guarantee of $750,000 yearly to cover expenses, the National Pro-Am Youth Fund has been disbursing more money every year," says secretary/manager Carmel Martin, Jr., a Monterey attorney who has served in his post since 1975. Currently, some 130 organizations a year will receive grants averaging $3,000 each.

The fund gives support with these priorities: youth welfare groups; schools and related educational activities; health services; and cultural activities. Types of youth organizations eligible for grants include those helping the retarded and handicapped, private and public schools, youth centers,

Little League, Babe Ruth League, Pony League, Pop Warner League, junior symphony, music, theater, opera, art, Boy and Girl Scouts, YMCAs, and YWCAs. In addition, the Youth Fund is now contributing to medical research and drug counseling for youngsters.

There are scholarships at the secondary and college level, which are living memorials of this tournament and its illustrious past. Young people are given an opportunity to become better citizens, and they in turn help other people. There are scholarships at Golden Gate University and a golf scholarship at San Diego State.

"The money is not only for youth, but help is provided to adults who are going back to school. Support is given Meals on Wheels for the seniors, Special Olympics, the Gateway Center, organizations for the blind and handi-

In 1987 the National Pro-Am Youth Fund will distribute a half-million dollars to youth groups, cultural organizations, and the handicapped. Participating here are Mary Kay Higgins, York School trustee; Paul St. Amour, York School student; Richard A. Lidstad, vice-president/3M Corporation; and Carmel C. Martin, Jr., secretary/trustee of the Youth Fund.

capped, the Carmel Bach Festival, and the Lyceum. A lot of help is brought to a lot of people."

The fund remembers Dan Searle, president from its inception until his death in 1983. The current National Pro-Am Youth Fund board of trustees, in addition to secretary Martin, is Ted Durein, president; Leon Edner, vice-president; and members John Burns, Warner Keeley, Charles Vout, Marshia Searle-Brown, Peter J. Coniglio, and Frank Thacker.

ROBERT TALBOTT TIES, INC.

The visitor entering the world of Robert Talbott Ties, Inc., is instantly transported into a dream. Imagine a redwood office building with spacious skylights, high ceilings, exposed beams, original oil paintings, antiques, rich colors, and plants everywhere—a warm, bright, comfortable artist's studio surrounded by Monterey cypresses and lush greenery. Then step into the private office of Robert Talbott himself, chairman and cofounder of the company with his wife, Audrey, a gentleman who spreads his arms expansively and says, "It's a dream come true!"

Robert Talbott, "Bob" to his friends, is having the time of his life, feeling fit and not even thinking about retirement. Bushy white eyebrows accent his sparkling eyes, and when he speaks about Talbott Ties, he weaves a classic Horatio Alger story with booming good humor. His son Robb brought out the family's first bottling of aged Chardonnay wine in late 1985, and Talbott provides jobs for 200 people in his gracefully beautiful plant,

where all the workers' areas are enhanced by art, antiques, and light, airy spaces.

It can be fairly said that Robert Talbott Ties are the highest-quality, top-of-the-market neckwear in the country, if not the world. They got that way because Talbott followed a consistent philosophy of manufacturing only the finest goods and spurning all temptations to venture into the mass market or sacrifice quality for lower price. "If you do something better than anybody else," he muses, "you've just got to stick to your guns, never cut corners, don't go after volume, don't worry about getting rich, and sooner or later you'll succeed!"

But he didn't make it without stumbling once or twice along the way, and in the end it was the teachings of his favorite Harvard Business School professor, General Georges Doriot, that formed the basis of his approach to manufacturing. Bob Talbott can trace his roots back to one Richard Talbott, who landed on the Maryland shore from England in 1653 and took up the profession of a vintner, farming 1,000 acres of grapes. The new Talbott Vineyards of Carmel Valley continues

Robert "Bob" Talbott (right), who cofounded Talbott Ties with his wife, Audrey (center). Their son Robb (left) brought out the family's first bottling of aged Chardonnay wine in late 1985.

a 335-year-old family tradition, but when Bob left Harvard in 1931, the Depression was ravaging America and the only job he could land was pumping gas in San Diego for $80 a month.

"Well, times were hard and there were no jobs in the East, but after a year of pumping gas you can imagine how I jumped at an offer from John Cowles to work for the *Register-Tribune* in Des Moines, Iowa, for $400 a month. I'd grown up in Iowa and went to Grinnell College there. I loved newspaper work, but I had two friends at the *Register-Tribune* who were also students of General Doriot's at Harvard, and we all wanted to get into manufacturing to put his ideas to use."

His first venture wasn't ties at all, but dog food. Vitarex Dog Food, to be

The original home of Robert Talbott Ties, Inc.

precise, the first dog food fully packed with vitamins. Bob and his partners set up shop in Tacoma, Washington, buying their raw meat from Armour and Swift, and at the outset were too poor to advertise so they "demonstrated" their dog food at supermarkets on the weekends. "We'd open up cans of our competitors' dog food and our own. In those years most dog food was a gray and yellowy color, unappetizing, but ours was pink—because we added food colors in it. Heck, we'd spread Vitarex on crackers and eat it ourselves. Within three years we were the best-selling dog food in the Pacific Northwest, but Armour and Swift also made dog food and they simply cut us off from our raw supplies."

Talbott returned to New York defeated, but he remembered the three principles of successful manufacturing that Professor Doriot had emphasized: Have three years' capital available, and don't spend more than a third of it a year; always control your raw material supply; and be prepared to work hard for little return for a long time. From 1935 to 1950 Talbott pursued a successful career as an insurance executive, but the dream never died.

During those years Audrey began making original silk bow ties for Bob at their home in New Canaan, Connecticut, and strangers on the commuter trains were always asking Bob where they could buy one like his. Audrey began turning out ties as a cottage industry, and the couple moved to Carmel in 1950 and launched into the business. It took 20 years for Robert Talbott Ties, Inc., to reach sales of one million dollars a year, but in each of those years the firm did better than in its previous annual period. "We never sold our receivables, which can get a lot of small companies in trouble, and we never sacrificed our quality. Eventually we made four-in-hands, long ties, ascots, accessories, card cases, watchbands, cloth belts, ladies' hats—at one time, 147 different products in all—all of them of higher quality and more expensive than our competition's. But when you're operating at the very top, you really have no competition," he says.

Talbott's first retail outlet opened in Carmel by the Sea, across from the Pine Inn, and the company now has four retail tie stores around the Monterey Peninsula. "We're one of the few manufacturers who do retail," Bob says. "We use our stores to test market reactions to new products. We don't need marketing surveys and expensive advertising; since 1976 we've been on an allocation basis, with our sales reps providing just the number of items a store can expect to sell. And we don't sell to department stores, just fine specialty shops. We've always known that the mass market would kill us. When you adopt this approach of quality—no matter what the product—and stay with it, you'll eventually have

The Monterey headquarters of Robert Talbott Ties, Inc.

more business than you can handle."

Bob Talbott's ties are traditional, even conservative—the classic Ivy League tie. Despite changing trends and fads, there has always been a demand for this formal garnishment, and Audrey's original designs and applications of themes from major artists have made it distinctive and crisp. Indeed, Talbott ties stand above the rest and Bob and Audrey's story is an inspiration to entrepreneurs. Creativity, rather than a get-rich-quick philosophy, has been the cornerstone of the firm's endurance and success. "We started out with no interest in making big money, only in creating the best-quality tie on the market," Bob says. "My son Robb learned the business from the bottom—crawling around under my desk. He now has a son who we hope will want to carry on in the business. We have a good name, and we've never cheapened it. And we're even back into vineyards after 300 years!"

The visitor leaves the dream of Robert Talbott Ties, Inc., still lost in the spell of riotous colors and fragrant blooms. The dream goes on and on, elegant and lovely, even hours apart from the place.

This interview was conducted prior to Bob Talbott's death on June 18, 1986.

COMMUNITY HOSPITAL OF THE MONTEREY PENINSULA

The healing power of the natural environment was harnessed in the design and construction of Community Hospital of the Monterey Peninsula to create a uniquely relaxed, noninstitutional setting.

When the private, not-for-profit hospital opened on its present site to much public acclaim in 1962, it was the only community hospital in the United States with all private patient rooms in an airy, garden environment.

The guiding philosophy of the hospital, reflected in its architectural design, is that people heal faster in pleasant, natural surroundings. So every patient room in the facility opens onto a patio or balcony and a view of the wooded hillside that slopes down to Monterey Bay.

Indeed, the first impression of

Community Hospital's original facility on Highway 1 in Carmel.

most people when they enter Community Hospital—with its gently splashing lobby fountain, its lush floral gardens, and large bubble skylights—is that they have entered a nice hotel, rather than a hospital.

"People deserve the dignity of privacy, regardless of their ability to pay," Community Hospital president Thomas E. Tonkin told *Look* magazine in 1964.

Community Hospital has so successfully combined aesthetics with prudent management that it has been able to keep per-patient costs below the average of costs at comparable Northern California hospitals. The hospital has also managed to maintain a relatively low debt ratio and a healthy financial footing.

The hospital has a consistently high occupancy rate, and even attracts patients from outside the Monterey Peninsula. Its health is boosted not only

by enthusiastic support from the people of the Monterey Peninsula but also by its dedicated auxiliary, which has 450 active volunteers and several thousand associate members.

Community Hospital (and the Community Hospital Foundation, which also owns and operates The Community Hospital Recovery Center) originated with a $500,000 endowment in 1927 by the late Grace Deere Velie, a local resident who was heiress to the John Deere tractor fortune.

At the suggestion of her personal physician, Dr. R.A. Kocher, she decided to endow a metabolic clinic for patients with nutritional diseases, and in 1930 the Grace Deere Velie Metabolic Clinic opened off Highway 1 in Carmel, site of the current Carmel Convalescent Hospital.

However, by March 1934, during Depression days, the fledgling hospital

was nearly forced to close its doors. Dr. Kocher assembled 18 Monterey and Carmel physicians who formed a cooperative to keep the clinic alive by converting it into a community hospital.

In the postwar prosperity of 1955, hospital trustees hired famed architect Edward Durell Stone to fashion a new facility on the present wooded site between Carmel and Monterey. The community's need for hospital beds had outgrown the Highway 1 site.

The 22-acre site for the new hospital facility was donated by the Del Monte Properties Corporation, at the personal direction of then-president Samuel F.B. Morse. Two-thirds of its $3.5-million cost was raised from supportive community members and the new hospital opened its doors in 1962. Architect Stone's design won the Governor's Award for Excellence in Architecture.

In 1971, thanks to continued generous support from the community which raised half of the $4-million cost,

the hospital expanded from 100 to 172 rooms and added a Mental Health Center. The dome over the fountain was also added at that time. Community Hospital now has a staff of over 200 physicians, 300 nurses, and 450 skilled support personnel. It operates a 24-hour emergency room and treats 10,000 inpatients and 100,000 outpatients each year.

The Community Hospital Foundation acquired the former Eskaton Monterey Hospital in 1982 and unveiled long-range plans to renovate the downtown Monterey landmark. Renamed Monterey Peninsula Hospital, the facility served as an overflow facility from Community Hospital until its conversion in 1985 to a comprehensive regional drug and alcohol treatment center, known as The Community Hospital Recovery Center.

In 1983 the Outpatient Pavilion opened at Community Hospital, providing much-needed space for outpatient services.

Hospital facilities now include a

Interior view of Fountain Court in the main lobby of Community Hospital on its Holman Highway site. The Holman Highway facility was constructed in 1962 and the dome was added over the Fountain Court in 1971.

clinical laboratory with a blood component therapy center, a radiation department with two linear accelerators and a computerized axial tomographic head and body scanner, six operating rooms, three emergency operating rooms, a mental health center, a pharmacy equipped with a computer to determine interaction of drugs, a rehabilitative therapy department, two delivery rooms, three nurseries, an oncology unit, and a 10-room cardiac care and intensive care unit. A new Outpatient Surgery Center was opened in 1987.

These facilities are especially valued by a community where the proportion of residents 65 years old or older is considerably higher than the national average, and is projected to increase by 20 percent by 1995.

SARDINE FACTORY RESTAURANT

Ted Balestreri's offices in a restored Spanish adobe overlooking Cannery Row feature a picture-postcard view of Monterey Bay, the aquarium, and gleaming shops and hotels, as well as Ted's and his partner's world-renowned Sardine Factory Restaurant. But Cannery Row, the street made famous by John Steinbeck, wasn't always pretty and attractive to tourists. A decade past, it was run-down and abandoned, lined with rusting former canneries. Today it's a mecca for visitors from all over the world.

Ted Balestreri and his partner were a moving force in this renovation. Their Cannery Row Company owns approximately 70 percent of the row, and the Sardine Factory was one of the first fine restaurants there when it opened on October 2, 1968. The enduring popularity of the restaurant is a testament to Ted Balestreri's and partner Bert Cutino's perseverance and constant evolution in tastes. "To stay on top, the most important ingredient is a sense of urgency. Complacency leads to downfall," Balestreri says. "We're constantly trying to improve our operation. One of the main reasons for our success is our staff of dedicated, well-trained personnel," Balestreri says.

Many others have noted Ted's enormous success. He is the immediate past president and chairman of the board of the National Restaurant Association, the highest elected office in the restaurant industry. He is a recipient of the IFMA Gold Plate Award, and the winner of the American Academy of Achievement Golden Plate Award, the highest recognition paid to a food-service operator by other leaders of the industry, as well as the first commissioner of tourism in California, appointed by Governor George Deukmejian.

The Balestreri family came to California in 1929 and was originally in the produce business. Ted started in the restaurant business at the age of 16

Ted J. Balestreri (left) and Bert P. Cutino, partners in Monterey's world-renowned Sardine Factory Restaurant.

as a busboy at the Highlands Inn, and by 19 years of age was the maitre d' and manager of the Seven Pleasures nightclub in Monterey—having claimed to be 23. "The happiest moments of my life were when Velma agreed to marry me, and my two sons, Teddy and Vinnie were born. My family is very important to me. Much of my success and happiness I attribute to my wife and family. This community has been so good to me that I want to give back some of what I have received." Ted has served as president of both the California Restaurant Association and the Monterey Peninsula Hotel & Restaurant Association, and sits on numerous boards of educational organizations that assist young people desiring a career in the food-service industry.

"We are dedicated to rebuilding Cannery Row nostalgically, to retain the flavor of old Monterey as Steinbeck memorialized it. We developed with sensitivity as we're committed to spend our lives and raise our families here," he adds.

In addition to the Sardine Factory, Ted and Bert own the Gold Fork in Carmel, the Rogue restaurant on Monterey's Fisherman's Wharf, the San Simeon restaurant near Hearst Castle, and a chain of Wendy's fast-food restaurants in Northern California.

"Diversification is the key to our success," he explains. "But the most important ingredient for this success is the partnership that made much of what we have achieved possible. Bert and I owe a great deal to our partners George Zarounian and Harry Davidian, whose loyal support and guidance helped us achieve our dreams. You have to believe in yourself. There is an old saying: 'A man who says he never had a chance never *took* a chance!' We believe no one coasts uphill; we keep growing and looking for new opportunities."

Bert P. Cutino met Ted Balestreri while both were students at Monterey Peninsula College. Born in Monterey in 1940, Bert is the son of a fisherman and like Ted got his start in the restaurant business at the bottom rung, as a

dishwasher at Holman's Guest Ranch in Carmel Valley. "We both started from the low end, but I saw no future in fishing," Bert says. "I used to go commercial fishing with my dad, who knew John Steinbeck and described him as 'some writer who really won't amount to anything,' " he laughs.

As co-owner of the Sardine Factory, and a partner in the Cannery Row Company and associated enterprises, Bert is in charge of managing the culinary end of the business, and keeping abreast of the many sophisticated evolutions of the public taste and trends in food. He's also a professional chef and western regional vice-president of the American Culinary Federation, the national chefs' organization. "We were the first to serve abalone, and we initiated regional cooking for the flavor of all this Cannery Row history. Our menu concept relates to that," he adds.

A visit to the Sardine Factory is like stepping through the pages of history itself. The entrance leads into the Cannery Row Room, decorated with photos and clippings of the row at the height of Steinbeck's and Doc Ricketts' era. A second room boasts a turn-of-the-century look with antique furniture and a Brunswick bar that was shipped around Cape Horn in 1900.

The Captain's Room features a nautical ambience complete with authentic sea captains' portraits and artifacts, while the Conservatory opens the diner's prospects to sunlight, a sparkling fountain, and leafy gardens. Step down into the basement to find the magnificent Wine Cellar room, with gold service for 26 at a long refectory table and 65,000 bottles of fine wine in one of America's finest wine cellars.

This is a grand setting for the epicurean delights awaiting the guests from the menu. Abalone cream bisque, local Monterey calamari, Salinas lettuce, Castroville artichokes, and other regional favorites are always featured, but the menu is continually evolving to reflect changing tastes and trends. "Our customers are more sophisticated today; they are more knowledgeable about wines and are often amateur chefs themselves. People are looking for lighter, more flavorful and exciting foods. They are more conscious of their health, desiring foods low in fat and sodium but still exciting to the palate. Today the special is the star of our menu, and our chefs are required to take 30 hours of nutrition education. We're constantly striving to stay ahead of the game; and our improvement is timeless, not a gimmick or fad," Bert says.

The magnificent Wine Cellar room, with gold service for 26 and 65,000 bottles of fine wine in storage.

Ted and Bert manage hundreds of well-trained, dedicated staff who have contributed much to their success. "Our employees have been faithful; and our success is closely linked to their success. We've enlarged three times, rebuilt after a fire, expanded the kitchens. We sacrificed much to improve, and we continue to seek improvement. In the United States, you still have the opportunity to become whatever you desire to be, and some of our culinary institute graduates can be chefs here sooner than in Europe. Today there are more educational opportunities available for those who desire a career in food-service. Years ago, a chef's base lasted longer, but in today's world this industry is one of the fastest growing in the country and is in a constant state of growth and change," says Bert.

"We kept our heritage and kept striving. We could see years ago that down the line this area would prosper," he adds.

And so it has, under the stewardship of Bert Cutino and Ted Balestreri.

CAMPOS AIR & OCEAN, INC.

Hermanehildo "Hilo" Campos and his wife, Joan, didn't know what they were getting into that fateful day in 1961 when a cousin persuaded them to use the family pickup truck to make a few extra dollars delivering air freight packages. Hilo was employed in the sand division of Del Monte Properties Co. and also delivered merchandise from the Sears catalog.

"There were only two air carriers in Monterey at the time, United and Pacific airlines," Hilo relates. "We started out delivering only one to three packages a day." He kept his Sears job until 1963 and stayed with Del Monte Properties eight years beyond that.

Today Campos Air & Ocean, Inc., has a fleet of 27 vehicles and 15 to 17 employees, depending on the season, and ships thousands of packages every week by air, surface, and ocean liner. All three of Joan and Hilo's children work in the family business, and this vivacious couple is looking forward to an active retirement with plenty of travel.

The Campos family came to Monterey in 1926, and lived in the Tortilla Flats neighborhood made famous by John Steinbeck's novel. Nicholos Campos, Hilo's father, rode with Pancho Villa in old Mexico; Nicholos' sword hangs over the family fireplace. Joan's roots go back six generations in Texas. As a boy, Hilo sold stray cats (at 25 cents each) to the legendary Doc Ricketts for his experiments.

Joan and Hilo married in 1951, and had children Frank, Jodie, and Herman IV exactly five years apart. Hilo built their comfortable Del Rey Oaks home himself, constructing a fireplace so magnificent that actress Kim Novak once asked him to build one for her. The couple have met numerous celebrities while delivering packages— they have fond memories of Paul Anka, Clint Eastwood, Dean Martin, and singer Charlie Pride, whose autographed picture graces their mantel.

The Campos family operated the delivery service out of their home until 1980, when they purchased their commodious warehouse in Sand City. "We delivered packages seven days a week, we brought people their lost luggage at 2 a.m. on Christmas Eve," Joan recalls. "Our daughter Jodie was driving a truck at the age of 14. And we haven't had a family vacation since the Seattle World's Fair!"

"We have a good word-of-mouth reputation," Hilo says. "Everybody knows we do a good job. We considered TV advertising but we don't really need it, we've got so much business already. My youngest son is the president of our sales division. And we have friends whose kids want nothing to do with their family business."

Since 1980 Campos Air & Ocean has outgrown its warehouse and purchased the adjacent Sand City lot and a $50,000 radio base that can track its drivers as far north as Oakland. "As a courtesy to CBS TV, we let them park their trailers here during the AT&T Tournament," Joan says.

Hilo and Joan could tell a thousand stories about their 26 years in the trucking business. Mostly, they're looking forward to seeing the world on a luxury cruise!

The Camposes are active in the Monterey Elk and Moose Lodge, and serve on the Horse Show Commitee for the Monterey County Fair and Exposition.

Top row (left to right): Hermanehildo "Hilo" Campos III, founder, with Tommy and Jodie Campos Adam. In the bottom row (left to right): Frank Campos, Joan Campos, who cofounded the firm with husband Hilo, and Herman Campos IV.

USA HOSTS MONTEREY

The entrance room behind Carol Chorbajian's office in downtown Monterey attests to a wealth of hospitality for visitors. Cases of wine, scenic calendars, brochures, and tourist route maps are stored there for USA Hosts Monterey, the local office of the second-largest destination management company in the nation. Just as the name suggests, Carol and her staff of four full- and 25 part-time people are professional hosts to some 75,000 visitors annually on the Monterey Peninsula.

USA Hosts, with corporate headquarters in Las Vegas, Nevada, started as Holiday Night Club Tours in 1961, taking vacationers around to the nightlife and sights of the City by the Bay. The business expanded to include basic tour and travel packages, offering bus trips around California, then branched out into the convention and meetings business. The Monterey office opened in 1978, and within three years the company acquired San Francisco Hosts and Jordan Leisure in Hawaii, to become USA Hosts in April 1982.

Chorbajian, now general manager, started as a tour guide with USA Hosts while a student at Monterey Institute of International Studies, where she was in the process of earning a master's degree in intercultural communications. She was called upon to translate and interpret for groups of French-speaking convention attendees and their spouses. "We still call M.I.I.S. and the Defense Language Institute for student translators," she says, but she personally handles the translation position for VIPs such as the president of American Motors Company's Renault Division.

USA Hosts both interacts with and acts as meeting planners. In its business the firm deals with three basic types of groups: associations on the national as well as regional levels, holding meetings and trade shows; corporate groups, including sales meetings and retreats;

and incentive programs, rewarding employees who exhibit outstanding productivity with an all-expense-paid trip to the Monterey Peninsula.

Working with these groups leads Chorbajian and her able assistants into all kinds of new adventures. They once had to provide clowns to IBM to accompany a tiger act from Marine World/Africa USA. On another last-minute request, they had to find a Lear jet to fly a corporate president to an important meeting in Pontiac, Michigan.

Golf is certainly the Peninsula's major attraction from the incentive standpoint. The courses are widely recognized as the finest in the land. "Golf, tennis, helicopter tours of the Big Sur coastline, wine tasting, and hot air ballooning are all very popular with our groups," Chorbajian says. USA

Hosts' largest clients include AT&T (all ground transportation arrangements for the annual Pro-Am Golf Tournament) and the California State Bar Association, which has held its annual convention three times in Monterey.

"We find that our lower room rates and many convention facilities have given us the edge over San Francisco," she concludes. USA Hosts also does a substantial amount of volunteer work in cooperation with the Monterey Peninsula Chamber of Commerce and Visitors and Convention Bureau.

Whether it's whale watching on the bay, evening dinners and theme parties, or air and hotel arrangements, USA Hosts Monterey is ready to accommodate groups of all sizes.

PEBBLE BEACH COMPANY

The pool and bathhouse at the Del Monte Hotel. Photo circa 1905

To write the full, rich history of Pebble Beach Company would require a book of its own. The world-famous resort and private enclave known as Pebble Beach (or, variously, the Del Monte Forest) is more than just a business. It's a residential community covering 5,300 acres, with 74 miles of privately maintained roads, 2,600 families, seven major golf courses, some of the most spectacular coastline in California (including the celebrated Lone Cypress overlooking the Pacific), and the luxurious Lodge at Pebble Beach and Inn at Spanish Bay, all along the renowned 17-Mile Drive.

The true historical antecedent to the Pebble Beach Company was the old Hotel Del Monte in Monterey, opened in 1880. Accommodating 500 guests and costing one million dollars to build, it created the 17-Mile Drive, first traveled as a stagecoach trip through Pacific Grove, Pebble Beach, south to the Carmel Mission, and back to Monterey. In 1908 the Pebble Beach Lodge, made of pine logs, was built as a stopover place for people taking this round-trip tour.

In February 1919 the Del Monte Properties Company (the predecessor of Pebble Beach Company) was formed by Samuel F.B. Morse and his financial backer, Herbert Fleishacker. It in-cluded the Hotel Del Monte, Pebble Beach Lodge (renamed the Del Monte Lodge), and 7,000 acres of choice land, and cost $1.3 million. S.F.B. Morse, grandnephew of the inventor of the telegraph, became the self-styled "Duke of Del Monte" for the ensuing half-century.

He loved horses, sailing, and golf, and oversaw the opening of the first Pebble Beach golf course in 1919. It was followed by the Cypress Point course in 1928 and the Spyglass Hill course in 1966. The AT&T National Pro-Am Tournament (formerly the Crosby) plays here, as do other prestigious tournaments, including the U.S. Opens in 1972, 1982, and soon, in 1992.

"When Herbert Fleishacker was obliged to go through bankruptcy, due to the Great Depression," Morse himself wrote, "I purchased a substantial amount of his stock and was placed in the position of control." His Del Monte Properties Company donated its waterfront acreage in Pacific Grove to the city, on the condition it remain open space, and in 1930 sold its Monterey County Water Works (now the California-American Water Co.).

Morse wrote, "The sale of our Water Company put us in a position to retire all our debts . . . so that we sailed through the worst period of the Depression."

The Del Monte Forest grew in reputation as one of the world's finest and most lavish resort and residential communities, as well as one of the most exclusive. Tollgates were constructed and the general public was charged for the use of the 17-Mile Drive. "The importance of charges at the gates," Morse continued, "is perhaps not appreciated by all. . . . Because of them there is available to local inhabitants and to the world one of the greatest private parks in existence. Without the charges . . . the area would have become like most of the rest of the waterfront on the California coast, uncontrolled and spoiled."

In 1946, with the sale of the Hotel Del Monte in Monterey to the U.S. Navy, the firm moved its hotel operations to Pebble Beach. Today the old Hotel Del Monte is the site of the Naval Postgraduate School. The price at the time was about two million dollars.

The organization continued to give parcels of its land "in perpetuity" as "open space undeveloped and accessible to the public. A great deal (of

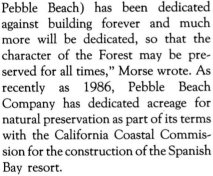

Entrance to The Lodge at Pebble Beach.

by *Monterey Peninsula Herald* "Peninsula Life" editor Anne Germain.

The Pebble Beach Foundation was incorporated in 1975 to raise funds for distribution to educational, social service, youth, cultural, and other nonprofit and charitable organizations on the peninsula. The foundation also supports the Del Monte Forest Foundation, which carries on Morse's dedication to the preservation and maintenance of open space.

The annual Pebble Beach Concours d'Elegance, considered by some to be the most prestigious of all concours, is one of several events that raise funds for the United Way of the Monterey Peninsula and Pebble Beach Foundation charities such as the Alliance on Aging, the Blind Service Center, the Hospice of the Monterey Peninsula, and the Monterey County Symphony Guild. The Pebble Beach Foundation is now distributing about $50,000 each year, and has made major contributions to the celebrated Monterey Bay Aquarium for acquisition of bird, fish, and plant life for the Sandy Shores Exhibit.

In 1977 Del Monte Properties Company changed its name to Pebble Beach Corporation (now Pebble Beach

Company) and was incorporated in Delaware. The following year the Del Monte Lodge changed its name to The Lodge at Pebble Beach. On May 1, 1979, 20th Century Fox Film Corporation completed its purchase of the company and became the parent corporation.

Fox made two major changes in 1981. In June, it merged with a company controlled by Marvin Davis and his family, and in September it formed a joint venture with Aetna Life and Casualty. Aetna's wholly owned subsidiary, Urban Diversified Properties Inc., was named to operate the Pebble Beach Company with Fox and Aetna as equal partners. At the end of 1983 Davis created a partnership (MKDG II) with Myron Miller, Thomas Klutznick, and Gerald Gray, which purchased the 50-percent interest originally sold to Aetna.

By November 1987 the company expects to employ about 1,200 people, making it the area's largest private employer, second overall only to the U.S. military. Its success hasn't changed the spectacular topography and serene coastal views that make Pebble Beach the special place it is.

The original "log" lodge in Pebble Beach. Photo circa 1909

Pebble Beach) has been dedicated against building forever and much more will be dedicated, so that the character of the Forest may be preserved for all times," Morse wrote. As recently as 1986, Pebble Beach Company has dedicated acreage for natural preservation as part of its terms with the California Coastal Commission for the construction of the Spanish Bay resort.

Golf courses in Pebble Beach are also considered open space and cannot be developed. The largest parcels of natural forest remaining in Pebble Beach are the 83.9-acre S.F.B. Morse Botanical Reserve and the 73.5-acre Pescadero Canyon property near the Carmel border, both deeded in perpetuity to the Del Monte Forest Foundation.

Morse died on May 10, 1969, 50 years after he founded the business. Many of his glory years are detailed in the book *Pebble Beach, The Way It Was*

GEYER CONSTRUCTION, INC.

Although he's a modest man who wouldn't brag of it, Peter V. Geyer can be said to have the finest ocean view from one of the choicest pieces of real estate in Monterey. He is the president of Geyer Construction, Inc., General Contractor, which owns the office building at the corner of Foam and David, directly facing the new aquarium and the Monterey Bay.

It started in January 1929 with Pete's father, Harold C. Geyer. The Great Depression was around the corner as Harold got his first contracting job, building the parking garage of the downtown Hotel San Carlos. When the San Carlos was demolished in 1981 to make way for the Monterey Sheraton, Harold saw his handiwork of 50 years earlier torn down. He had retired in 1971 and died on December 21, 1984.

Harold Geyer spent the 1930s and 1940s building quality residences all over the Peninsula. Geyer Construction's first office outside of the family home was in the historic adobe that is now the Sancho Panza restaurant on Pacific Street. The 1950s saw the company operating out of "an old house converted to office space at 787 Munras Avenue," reminisces Dorotha "Dottie" Emery, secretary/treasurer, who has been with the firm since August 1951. The "old house" is now the headquarters of Pacific Bell.

Harold Geyer was instrumental in getting the Carpenters' Apprenticeship Program established in the state of California. He felt the program was keenly needed and time has proven it to be a highly successful and productive one.

It was 1960 when Geyer Construction moved to Del Monte Avenue near the old Railway Express office. In 1971 the firm acquired its present office quarters located at the corner of David Avenue and Foam Street in Monterey. Along the way the company was incorporated, in 1962, with Harold, Peter, Dottie, and Louis A. Souza

as officers. Souza began working for Harold in 1946 as an apprentice out of high school, and is vice-president of the corporation today.

The war years saw Geyer Construction busily at work at Camp Roberts and Fort Ord. Peacetime brought the challenge of building the first structures for Monterey Peninsula College. "We were responsible for the original MPC campus, starting in 1948," Pete says. "My dad brought in buildings from Watsonville, salvaged from an abandoned Army base used in World War II." The firm has since done much of the renovation work at the college, and it built the acclaimed MPC Theater, the premier facility for live theater on the Peninsula, in 1969.

During the years when fishing was good on the Row, the firm built and rebuilt the canneries. Then in the 1950s and 1960s the Monterey Peninsula went into a real building boom, and Geyer Construction was in the heart of the action.

With the population on the Central Coast increasing rapidly, construction of new schools was a high priority. Geyer Construction built Seaside High School (1963), Portola Junior High in Seaside (1965), MPC's Physical Science and Life Science Building (1967), Gavilan College Phase II in Gilroy (1968), and academic facilities at the Naval Postgraduate School (1969). It built portions of Monterey High School, Carmel High School, Carmel Woods School, and the first phase of the final Pacific Grove High School. In later years it constructed the Walter Colton Middle School in Monterey and the Martin Luther King School in Seaside.

From the mid-1960s through the 1970s, the building emphasis shifted away from schools and toward banks, savings and loans, and office buildings. The company was responsible for the main branch in downtown Monterey and the Carmel and Carmel Valley branches of Monterey Savings and

Loan, and new offices of Valley National Bank (now Household), Security Pacific Bank, Bank of America, and Great Western Savings. It won the contract to build the Mid Valley Shopping Center in Carmel Valley and saw the project to completion in 1966.

The company also completed some of the Peninsula's most ambitious building projects of the 1970s. These included the terminal annex at the Monterey Peninsula Airport (1974) and the new U.S. Coast Guard Station (1977). Begun in the 1970s and finished in 1980 were the Garden West Office Plaza on Garden Road in Monterey, Triple Tree Properties office complex in Carmel, and Bob's Big Boy Restaurants in Salinas and Monterey.

Approaching its 60th year in the 1980s, Geyer Construction, Inc., has already remodeled the Longview Buildings at Asilomar State Park in Pacific Grove and completed construction of the Carmel Center professional offices in Carmel Rancho, the 337 Eldorado office complex in Monterey, and the Way Station motel and restaurant adjacent to the airport.

No other local general contractor can match the number of projects Geyer Construction has built over the years. The company employs between 10 and 50 union workers based on their workload. "We haven't tried to be the biggest contractor, but we stress the quality of our work," he says. "Our reputation is based on quality construction."

The company has always operated as a tightly knit, cooperative group. Dottie comments, "We make every effort to take care of our clients' needs efficiently and in the most cost-effective manner. Our clients recognize that and come back, again and again."

Despite the present sewer moratorium and the water supply problems, and while the firm feels new construction will be minimal on the

Peninsula, Geyer anticipates a great
deal of remodeling will develop in both
the residential and commercial field. Of
course, new projects will develop in the
Salinas area and areas such as Ryan
Ranch. Geyer Construction will be
there, as always.

The company's motto is "Building
a tradition of quality since 1929." "My
dad, many times at his own expense,
adhered to that principle. In our industry, he was highly regarded as a man
of integrity, and he tried very hard to
always be fair. We want to continue to
operate in that manner," Pete says.

Harold C. Geyer (1901-1984), founder.

FIRST WATCH RESTAURANT

Down on the waterfront in Pacific Grove, where Ocean View Boulevard meets the Monterey Bay Aquarium and the Hopkins Marine Station commands its majestic view, sits the old American Tin Cannery building, once the granddaddy of the sardine trade, now home and hearth to the First Watch Restaurant.

The American Tin Cannery has seen its share of businesses come and go, including more than sardines, but the First Watch is an enduring success at that location, and has even given birth to a half-dozen new First Watches from here to Sarasota, Florida.

Founder John Sullivan was a new arrival in Monterey just five years ago, having come from Denver and a career that saw him rise from a dishwasher to vice-president of a chain of 67 restaurants. "I had grown tired of board meetings, stock analysts, the executive life," he remembers, "and wanted to move my family to Monterey because it's the best place to live. Life is too short to keep chasing bucks all the time."

When he found the Tin Cannery, the building had just come through extensive renovation by owner Ted Balestreri. Its high, slate-gray ceilings, flooded with sun from the skylights,

Shown here is the American Can Company building as it looked in 1939. The historic building is now the home of the First Watch Restaurant, opened in 1983. Courtesy, The Pat Hathaway Collection

presented an appealing warmth, spaciousness, and closeness to the ocean. Indeed, the Tin Cannery feels like an aquarium itself. The "First Watch" nautical theme merged perfectly with the restaurant's specialty: breakfast.

Opened in February 1983, the restaurant still serves eggs as its basic food, closes at 2:30 p.m. following lunch, offers no alcoholic beverages, absolutely guarantees the customer's satisfaction, doesn't advertise, and is almost always busy. Local people come back there, and bring their out-of-town guests, because the food is terrific and the service genuinely friendly. "This old building is alive again," Sullivan laughs.

"Attention," the menu gently reminds us, "Wasting a little time is healthy. It can also be very enjoyable, especially if you have a lot of real important stuff to do. Furthermore, we believe that your breakfast is the most important meal of the day."

"Our philosophy is that our people are what makes us successful. We try to provide jobs with self satisfaction and give our employees the outlets they need to grow. We have a very low turnover rate, pay comparably or better than other restaurants, and have never laid anybody off for lack of business. People enjoy working here," Sullivan says.

People certainly enjoy eating there, too. "We have a caliber of service you'd expect from a more expensive restaurant," Sullivan adds, "but we're sensitive to the average ticket and keep it down around five dollars a person."

With First Watches now open in Phoenix, Kansas City, San Mateo, Illinois, and Florida, Sullivan somehow manages to relax and extend his unique brand of hospitality from the American Tin Cannery in Monterey.

The old building, completely renovated in a nautical theme, invites guests to return time and again to enjoy the fine food and relaxed atmosphere.

McCORD & WALD

As you approach the offices of McCord & Wald, you sense immediately the special nature of the design business. The building is clad in genuine Carmel Stone, vintage 1915 or so, hand laid by one Manuel Real, a noted stonemason, on Eldorado Street in old Monterey. It was the home of the Real family before Jim McCord and David Wald moved their architecture, planning, and interior design firm in as the first commercial tenants. The exterior is old, classic; the interior is warmly modern, comfortable.

While it's fair to say that McCord & Wald has a special flair for the restoration of historic buildings, it's also important to note that the firm designs the interiors as well. Not all architects can do both.

The 10-year history of the firm (since 1977) shows an impressive dossier of architectural accomplishments, including land planning at Ryan Ranch Research Park, Williams Industrial Planned Unit Development in Sand City, corporate offices for Shearson American Express in Carmel, Small Business Reports in Del Rey Oaks, and Yates, Downer, Dyer and Kirkpatrick in the historic Perry House in Monterey. The firm has also provided design services for the expansion of the Circulation Department at the *Monterey Peninsula Herald*, The Tinnery Restaurant in Pacific Grove, and Gianni's Restaurant of Monterey, retail shops in older structures including Bittersweet (the Angwin Building, 1902) and Robert Talbott Ties' "Talbott-Carmel" shop (Court of the Golden Bough, circa 1920), many custom residences throughout the Monterey area, and many church facilities, including the recent interior renovation for the Church of the Wayfarer in Carmel.

Jim McCord and David Wald, partners in the business, offer their

A model of the Pacific Grove Cinema, currently under construction.

clients the assurance that every McCord & Wald project is handled by a principal. The company employs six architects in addition to Jim, and has additional technical and clerical staff to meet the varied demand of today's clients' needs. "We focus on projects relating to historical concepts," Jim says. "We find new uses for existing structures, or optimize the existing uses within."

One such project that McCord & Wald is quite proud of is the historic Miller Adobe, the last of its type built in Monterey, now utilized as a law office. Working with the State Parks Department, the owner, and the City of Monterey, Jim responded to the historical parameters generated by the existing structure "to preserve the charm of the building while making it more utilitarian." Jim adds, "We have a sensitivity to adobe construction, where the walls are curved and the ceilings low."

Another project was President Herbert Hoover's mother's hunting lodge, which dates from about 1905. This redwood structure on a two-plus-acre parcel in Monterey is now part of a condominium project designed to save the structure from the wrecker's ball. Instead, McCord & Wald and development partners acquired the property and defined a few small residences to share the site, all done in an "architecturally analo-

The Miller Adobe, the last of its type built in Monterey, was a McCord & Wald renovation project. (Although the building has wood siding, it is actually an adobe structure at the lower level.)

gous" design motif.

Two recent examples of McCord & Wald's genius for historical restoration are Mcdougall's Brass Rail restaurant in Salinas and Bittersweet coffee and confections inside the Angwin Building in Pacific Grove, a project of Jim's wife, Claudia.

Also in Pacific Grove, Jim, along with staff architect Ray Smith, has created a new cinema structure within the Victorian context of the downtown district. The sensitivity of the design was heralded by the citizens in a special election, in which the project was the only issue on the ballot. A high turnout and overwhelming "aye" approved the project.

McCord & Wald has expanded beyond the Monterey Peninsula, and now has offices in Palm Springs, where the firm sees the opportunity to use its expertise to help retain some of the special attributes of the desert architecture. Projects there include renovation work at the Palm Springs Hilton Riviera Hotel, and a variety of projects in the south Coachella Valley including a new fire station at La Quinta and a series of tennis resort condominiums at the historic La Quinta Hotel, circa 1926.

CARMEL VALLEY RANCH RESORT

Heading east along the Carmel Valley Road, visitors can look to the right and notice the lush sprawling golf course surrounded by the Santa Lucia Mountains. It is the Carmel Valley Ranch Resort, set on 1,700 of the most spectacular acres in California, and as of June 1987 it has extended its exclusive membership amenities to guests with a brand-new resort.

The Carmel Valley Ranch Resort boasts a rich history. Originally patented to Richard and Daniel Snively under the Homestead Act in 1876, the property was used as a dairy farm and included orchards of apricots, nectarines, and cherries, and almond trees. The ranch sold its produce to the Del Monte Hotel in its heyday as a tourist mecca.

Until 1953 the land was still in active use as a ranch, having pear orchards and fields for grazing cattle. Del Monte Properties acquired it in 1962, and Carmel-based Landmark Land Company, Inc., the current owners, bought the ranch in 1976 and started developing.

Some 200 families maintain private residences here, and the world-class golf and tennis clubs have always been reserved exclusively for members and their guests. With the grand opening of the resort, visitors are now able to enjoy all the amenities of this elegant setting.

This exclusive resort offers much more than any conventional hotel can. The casual atmosphere is relaxed and personal, luxurious but not stuffy. One hundred deluxe suites are located in 23 separate ranch-style buildings with soaring cathedral ceilings, warm views, and large private decks. Twelve of these also feature a private outdoor spa.

All the suites have at least one wood-burning fireplace; many have two. Color cable TVs with remote control and HBO are located in both the bedroom and living room of each suite. An honor bar and wet bar are included, and each suite has three phones and two phone lines. The extra-large bathrooms feature grand tubs and separate showers.

The unique rugs are hand woven in Hong Kong, the bed quilts hand sewn by Amish craftswomen, the china painted with floral designs by local Carmel artisans. Gracious touches abound, as one would expect from a resort of unsurpassed prestige.

The resort's meeting and banquet facilities and three restaurants are all designed for the most discriminating clientele. The lodge's massive stone fireplace serves as the focus of this magnificent building with its ballroom, 4,500 square feet of meeting space, two boardrooms, and—of course—the famous golf and tennis clubs.

Golf and tennis, enjoyed at Carmel Valley Ranch Resort to championship standards, remain the principal attractions. The resort houses a full staff of pros to help guests improve their game. Like Landmark's other hotels and resorts—La Quinta Hotel Golf & Tennis Resort, Mission Hills

Resort Condominiums, Palm Beach Polo and Country Club, and The Waterford Hotel—Carmel Valley Ranch Resort offers the finest life-style under the sun.

MONTEREY BAY TRIBUNE

Walk into the office of Neill Gardner, editor of the *Monterey Bay Tribune*, and he's likely to shake your hand, offer you a seat, and warn you, "Don't mess up my desk!" while gesturing toward a desktop littered with heaps of paperwork and photos. Have no fear, the veteran editor knows where every piece of copy belongs in the only newspaper on the Peninsula to be delivered by mail to all the homes in Pebble Beach.

The weekly *Tribune* traces its roots back to 1888, making it the oldest publication in the area. Despite several name changes and except for a 13-year hiatus between 1956 and 1969, the paper has been published with continuity. Editor Gardner himself traces his roots to Oregon and a colorful career as a newspaperman throughout the Pacific Northwest, before his arrival in Monterey in 1967.

Born as the *Pacific Grove Review* in 1888, the paper appeared daily in the 1910s, reverted to weekly during the Roaring 20s, and was rechristened the *Tribune* in 1946. It ceased operations in 1956 until it was revived by Gardner in 1969. "I'd come to Monterey to work for *The Herald*," he reminisces, "and every day when I drove home to Pacific Grove, I noticed the sign reading 'Population 12,000,' and thought it was the only town of that size without a weekly paper!"

"The first issue of the new *Tribune* was edited in my garage and pasted up on my dining room table," Gardner adds. "In 1969 the paper campaigned for an end to Prohibition in Pacific Grove, which was founded as a religious retreat and banned all alcohol sales; the campaign succeeded, by a narrow margin, but the town is still about 50/50 divided on the issue today," he says.

Gardner started a Marina edition of the *Tribune* in 1972, and sold both the Pacific Grove and Marina papers to David Lindsay of Sarasota, Florida, in 1976. Lindsay then added a Seaside edition in 1977, and sold the con-

glomerate of papers to Harry Casey of King City. Gardner and partner Lou Haddad reacquired the empire in 1983, and have consolidated it into today's *Monterey Bay Tribune*.

The lively weekly keeps its readers up to date on events around the Monterey Peninsula, and takes a firm editorial stand on current issues, no matter how controversial. Co-publisher and advertising manager, former Seaside Mayor Lou Haddad contributes his outlook in the "Point of Information" column. Gardner pens

weekly "Shore Lines," items from a seasoned reporter's notebook. Seaside Councilman Dan Quinn offers helpful information to vets in "Veterans Corner." An occasional columnist is Pacific Grove Mayor Morris Fisher, and *Tribune* readers are well known for expressing themselves freely and at length; the paper delights in publishing their letters.

With its circulation at 15,000, the *Monterey Bay Tribune* is a real force on the Peninsula as it sails into its second century.

MORE THAN 250 teachers, alumni and friends attended reunion of Oak Grove Elementary School (they called it Grammar School) in Monterey. From left: Recently retired Monterey Police Chief Harold Benadom (1927-36), Evelyn Diaz Hinckley (1926-35), Adele Duck, who started teaching in 1928; Mayoral Candidate Dan Albert (1927-36) and Pacific Grove businessman Monroe Schuetz.
WILL ROBINSON PHOTO

Monterey Bay Tribune

VOLUME 13, No. 33   MONTEREY, CALIFORNIA   THURSDAY, SEPTEMBER 4, 1986

Veterans enjoyed Martha Raye

By JON HAGAN

By 10:25 on an overcast Saturday morning at the Marina American Legion Post, an excited crowd of ex-paratroopers and their families had gathered. Gathered to wait for "Colonel Maggie" better known as Broadway and film star Martha Raye.

The color guard was drawn up near the entrance and the traditional red carpet was out. Colonel Hendrickson, the garrison commander at Fort Ord, was being briefed on the morning's ceremonies when the color guard commander, CSM Mike Collins, retired, from Antioch, cheerfully informed him that the inspection would be "just like it is in the Army, Sir." That

MARTHA RAYE and Legion of Valor member Jim Spitz shared a secret during third annual Airborne Reunion in Marina on Saturday. Raye celebrated her 70th birthday and 50 years in show business over weekend. She entertained troops in North Africa during World War Two, later in Vietnam and was wounded three times. Raye left her false teeth in Hollywood, so much-heralded raffle had to be called off, but she donated $1000 to the Airborne Association.

drew a laugh from the crowd as well as Collins' bringing the color guard to attention to salute two late-arriving paratroopers on motorcycles.

Raye wore Vietnam duds

Then, shortly after 10:30, a brown Cadillac pulled up to the red carpet and Martha Raye, in fatigue jacket and the beret she was awarded in Vietnam, was helped out. Lt. Col. Raye and Col. Hendrickson returned the salute of the color guard and Saturday's ceremonies at the All Services Airborne Drop-In were underway.

Hendrickson, a former paratrooper who served with the 101st Airborne, in addressing the ex-airborne soldiers, told them that while he cherished his years as a paratrooper, airborne units were no longer the fastest and most efficient troops to put in the field.

Hendrickson said that distinction now belongs to the light infantry divisions and the first of those, the first in the nation, the Seventh Infantry Division (Light) formed at Fort Ord had just passed its certification test in exercises at Fort Hunter Liggett.

He said the light division concept was developed for low- to mid-intensity wars like Vietnam and Korea and the purpose of the Division is to contain the level of the war at that intensity. He concluded his remarks by thanking Gen. William Harrison for not being able to attend the "Drop In" so that Hendrickson could be reacquainted with his former comrades.

She served in Africa

Martha Raye graciously signed autographs for the paratroopers and posed for countless pictures with them *Please see Page Three*

SOPRANO STEPHANIE MYSZAK, above, and jazz violinist Jeremy Cohen will be soloists at free Monterey Bay Symphony concerts at 1 p.m. on Saturday, Sept. 6 in Soledad and Sunday, Sept. 7 at 2 p.m. at Monterey County Fairgrounds. Cohen is a bay area native. He has played solo violin in many television movies and recorded albums with Ray Charles and Horace Silver. Myszak is the daughter of John Myszak, Forest Grove School instructor, now lives in New York City. A music major at

Seaside community clinic open house Sept. 10

Seaside Medical Clinic directors will host an open house at the new Seaside Community Medical Clinic, 1280 Broadway Avenue, Seaside, on Wednesday, Sept. 10 from 5 to 7 p.m.

The new facility will house ten clinic staff members and provide a broad range of services, including general medicine, obstetrics, gynecology, pediatrics, geriatrics, minor surgery and some emergency. The clinic provides quality comprehensive medical care to low income and disadvantaged people and provides one of the few obstetrical services available to Medi-Cal recipients on the Peninsula.

The directors and staff invite the community to tour the new facilities. Refreshments will be served.

Lions to hear lawmen

Seaside Lions Club has arranged a series of provocative programs and the public is urged to attend. The schedule: Sept. 4, Business Meeting; Sept. 11, Assemblyman Sam Farr; Sept. 18, Judge Michael Fields; Sept. 25

DOUBLETREE HOTEL

In 1972 a revised urban-renewal plan was drafted in Monterey; it called for a major luxury hotel and convention center to be built right at Fisherman's Wharf. Ground was broken for the Doubletree Hotel in 1976, and it opened within two years, the crown jewel in the Doubletree chain that was then located mainly on the West Coast. In 1988, as the Monterey Doubletree celebrates its 10th anniversary, the chain will have grown to include 25 upscale hotels nationwide.

The city had accurately predicted that the Fisherman's Wharf site would be attractive to conventions and groups. From the first, the Doubletree Hotel has catered to business gatherings, conferences, and conventions of out-of-town visitors, who enjoy the Monterey Peninsula's famed golf courses, spectacular scenery, new aquarium, and fine restaurants. Over 70 percent of the Doubletree's business is in hosting these groups. "It's fair to say that the Doubletree is the leading hotel for conventions visiting Monterey," says general manager Mark White.

The Doubletree professionals know how to make a business meeting both successful and memorable. The facility offers a Come Early, Stay Late privilege so that conventioneers can enjoy visiting the Peninsula for three days before and/or after their meeting at guaranteed group rates. The Doubletree Meeting Planner's Guarantee offers performance guarantees on all meeting rooms, audiovisual equipment, banquets, reservations, even coffee breaks, so that every detail of the convention is handled perfectly.

The Monterey Conference Center adjoining the hotel has facilities to handle any size meeting; and the hotel produces gourmet cuisine in the elegant Peter B's restaurant and rooftop Brasstree Lounge, with its panoramic bay views. Many of the 374 deluxe guest rooms, including 15 suites, come equipped with the same great views overlooking Fisherman's Wharf, Cannery Row, and the aquarium.

The Doubletree's decade-long history of prosperity has been an important part of Monterey's economic growth. The hotel itself has benefited from the Doubletree chain's industry innovations: STAR and Product Differentiation. The STAR program (Steps to Accent Recognition) teaches employees how to personally recognize and address both first-time and repeat guests, offer superior service, and sincerely thank guests for staying at a Doubletree hotel. The Product Differentiation Program includes special quick check-in and check-out plans to eliminate waiting, the five-minute breakfast service, and a bedtime snack of freshly baked chocolate chip cookies.

"The Doubletree guest really feels welcome in Monterey," White asserts. Monterey's Doubletree is one of only 35 hotels in the nation to be honored with the Gold Key Award from *Meetings and Conventions* magazine. The meeting planners themselves elected the Doubletree for this highest designation. With Monterey's rich history all around it, the Doubletree Hotel has made its first decade a great one.

Monterey's Doubletree Hotel, located in Portola Plaza and noted for its convention facilities, is one of 35 hotels in the nation to be honored with Meetings and Conventions *magazine's coveted Gold Key Award.*

THE CARMEL PINE CONE

It's arguably true that Carmel-by-the-Sea is the most famous small town in America, especially since box office heavyweight Clint Eastwood became mayor. It's also true that while other newspapers on the Monterey Peninsula may have larger circulations, or more ancient roots, *The Carmel Pine Cone* has been publishing without interruption for the longest number of years, and has reached a worldwide audience. It will observe its 75th anniversary in 1989.

That first issue, dated February 3, 1915, served due notice on the world that the village of Carmel had a voice: "Permit Us!" publisher William L. Overstreet opined, "We have come to stay." The paper reported on the popular movement to divide California into two states: some believed "the people of the southern part of the state are not true Californians." "Carmelians," on the other hand, "are gentle folks, polite in the best sense of the word," and the village itself is the most lovable spot in this fair land."

Noted local poet Herbert Heron put it this way:

> *The Carmel Pine Cone* bursts
> upon the scene,
> With youth and sap, with color, fruit, and all;
> Our local press, our weekly magazine . . .
> And every little while the Pine Cones Fall.

This particular *Pine Cone* falls (on the streets and desks of the village, in Carmel Valley and Big Sur) every Thursday morning. "And when Clint was running for mayor," editor Mac McDonald remembers, "it was all gone by Thursday afternoon."

The stock market crash of 1929 found Perry Newberry and Allen Griffin publishing the paper, with founder Overstreet having become Carmel postmaster. The crash itself went unreported, but the *Pine Cone* offered 100 shares in Santa Claus,

OUR 72ND YEAR, NO. 15   April 10, 1986

CLINT WINS

It's Eastwood, Laiolo and Fischer in landslide

By MICHAEL GARDNER

IN THE election heard around the world, it is no longer Clint Eastwood, the actor.

It is Clint Eastwood, the mayor of Carmel-by-the-Sea.

Eastwood, the world-famous actor known for his Dirty Harry and Man with No Name spaghetti western roles, overwhelmingly defeated incumbent Mayor Charlotte Townsend Tuesday night.

Eastwood, who will serve a two-year term for $200 monthly, will be sworn in April 15. Also swept into four-year terms on the Eastwood ticket were Elinor Laiolo, a former public school administrator; and Bob Fischer, the ex-assistant Carmel police chief who retired after 31 years of service in the department.

Laiolo and Fischer, who also will be sworn in next Tuesday, replace incumbents David Maradei and Robert Stephenson, both of whom served a single, four-year term.

Nearly three out of every four (73 percent) of the Carmel registered voters went to the polls, giving Eastwood a 2,166 to 799 margin of victory, according to unofficial results.

Environmental Party candidate Tim Grady finished with 31 while businessman Paul Laub, who dropped out of the race five days ago to support Eastwood, received six votes.

Eastwood's landslide win carried over into the council race where Laiolo garnered 1,896 votes with Fischer right behind at 1,850.

Maradei finished third at 635 and in fourth was Stephenson with 592 votes. They were followed by Tom May, 458; Anne Woolworth, 243; Don Lampson, 106; and Robert Weber, 79.

Townsend, Maradei and Stephenson formed a council whose reign had been marked by numerous achievements, failures and controversy.

Surely the achievements are considerable, ranging from a massive and speedy beach rehabilitation project, to completion of a pro-resident general plan to a complete renovation of city hall, both in personnel and structural remodeling.

But it is the disappointments that led to their downfall — the list of undone projects over four years is just as numerous as the tally of accomplishments.

Awaiting the new council are: Sunset Center parking, settlement of litigation concerning the Odello Ranch and Spanish Bay development, and which direction to go on the proposed Carmel River dam.

BUT MORE importantly, the overwhelming win is an indication that this town is ready for a change in attitude, or so says Eastwood.

Eastwood's key campaign theme has been

"bringing the community together" — a slogan he says was developed in response to concerns that the council was too highhanded in its dealings with the merchants in particular and residents in general.

Eastwood contends that the council lacked openness, fairness and an interest in dealing in a "neighborly way" rather than through "intimidation" and "high handedness."

Eastwood promises an open ear, pleases and thank yous in his dealings.

In an exclusive interview with the *Carmel Pine Cone/Carmel Valley Outlook* minutes after the results were announced, Eastwood talked about his first day's agenda, the campaign and the media hype that reached a climax Tuesday night with 200 journalists sardined into the Sunset Center press conference.

"I guess I feel good," Eastwood said. "I've campaigned long and hard. I've done 55 teas. It feels good. I got to meet an awful lot of people neighbors and exchange ideas. It makes me appreciate my community even more than I did."

Eastwood promised more public participation in the government, saying he wants to "take the government out of the hands of the few and put it into the hands of the many."

The city will use more of its "local talent" during the next two years instead of "high-priced" consultants.

On his first day's agenda, Eastwood includes "immediate" action on the proposed Sunset Center parking garage and addresses the traffic congestion problems in town.

The city, under his leadership, will join the Holman Highway Task Force and the assessment district to study the proposed Carmel River dam, he said.

City lawsuits against the county on the Odello, Spanish Bay and Mission Ranch developments will be analyzed, Eastwood said.

Eastwood promised to move "briskly ahead" on public restrooms at Devendorf Park (the council already has approved the design and construction is scheduled for summer). And he wants public restrooms at Piccadilly Park.

On the election of Fischer and Laiolo, Eastwood said, "It's just wonderful...We both feel the personal and neighborly aspects of local government could be better."

EASTWOOD said he was surprised by the margin of victory, adding that "I think it's good. An awful lot of people are advocating change. I think it's a culmination of the impersonal acts that have divastified people."

Asked whether his star status helped or hurt the campaign, Eastwood replied: "I have to admit that I was worried about the

Continued on page 3

CLINT EASTWOOD celebrates the news of his victory over Charlotte Townsend to become Carmel's new mayor. (Holly McFarland photograph.)

CARMEL MAYORAL RESULTS

Precinct	Townsend	Eastwood	Laub	Grady
Absentee	125	259	4	6
One	201	483	0	6
Two	179	494	1	6
Three	136	454	0	6
Four	158	476	1	12
Totals	799	2,166	6	31

Incorporated, to those who were "suspicious of the safety of stock market speculation." Author Lincoln Steffens gave a talk to the children in the school, and Carmel houses were advertised "under $5,000."

The onslaught of World War II brought total blackouts to the village. The *Pine Cone*, guided by Cliff and Wilma Cook, urged residents to stop making "needless" telephone calls at night. "All For One and One For All," the Cooks editorialized. On June 11, 1942, the paper absorbed its only competitor, the *Cymbal*, and called itself the *Pine Cone-Cymbal* through the 1960s.

The paper also introduced several

new journals. Its *Carmel Valley Outlook* was published separately from 1959 to April 1981, when it merged with the *Pine Cone*. The weekly entertainment and dining guide, *Monterey Peninsula Review*, was born in 1973 and still publishes today. Its focus goes beyond Carmel to all the towns on the Peninsula.

Current publisher Bill Brown of Brown & Wilson, Inc., acquired the *Pine Cone* from Al Eisner in 1982, and is thriving with 24 employees. Clint Eastwood's mayoralty hasn't hurt the paper a bit. In fact, guess who writes an occasional *Pine Cone* column? Yup. His Honor himself.

KIWANIS CLUB OF MONTEREY

Back in 1915, when the national Kiwanis Club organization was born in Michigan, the founders took the name from an Indian term, "nun-kee-wan-is." Loosely translated it means "we gather together, we make a big noise."

Well, nobody would accuse the Monterey Kiwanians of not honoring the spirit of the organization. These fellows make a big noise every Wednesday noon at the Elks Club, where they raise money for dozens of good causes and leave a tremendous impact on the community.

The Monterey Kiwanis is the second-largest club in the Cal-Nev-Ha district and in 1980 was awarded a rating among the three best clubs in the world. Chartered on October 23, 1925, the club boasted 41 original members including many of the Monterey Peninsula's leading citizens of the day. Since 1926 the club has sponsored 12 new clubs spanning from Gilroy in the north down to King City to the south. Make that 13 clubs if you include the 1978 sponsorship of Dandenong, Australia!

Over all those years perhaps the most outstanding Monterey Kiwanis member was the late past president, Fong Qua Jing. He singlehandedly organized 10 new Kiwanis clubs, was elected to the state organization's

Charlie Jett, Ted Neth, Cliff Ferris, and Steve Magyar (from left) with Miss Monterey County of 1964 in front of the Kiwanis Club's Corn Booth at the Monterey County Fair.

lieutenant governor's post, and "just didn't understand the meaning of the word 'no,'" club members fondly recall.

The Kiwanis have supported so many worthwhile charities that it's impossible to list them all here. Perhaps one of the club's premier achievements was its instrumental role in the founding of Monterey Peninsula College (MPC). In 1947, at a board meeting at the Casa Munras Hotel, club members led by Murray Vout decided that Monterey needed a community college "so that our kids wouldn't have to go all the way over to Salinas to continue their education." A bond issue and speaker's bureau helped raise funds, and the community rallied behind the club, which also lured Colonel Calvin Flint here as the first MPC president.

Another contribution of lasting value is the Tawes swimming pool at

George Dovolis, past president, dedicating the swimming pool at Dennis the Menace Park, 1963.

Dennis the Menace Park, dedicated in 1963 by past president George Dovolis. Club members like to remember the night they threw Clint Tawes into the pool at Fred Gardner's ranch in Carmel Valley as part of their celebration of the event. Generations of youngsters have enjoyed the facility at this world-famous playground.

The Monterey County Fair wouldn't be the same without the annual Kiwanis Corn Booth, which dates back as far as the fair itself. The Great Monterey Squid Festival is sponsored and run by the club. This annual event has been around since 1984.

At a recent Wednesday lunch meeting, director Harold Firstman of the Spaulding Pro Am Golf Tournament presented the club with a $15,000 check to be distributed to charity. The Monterey Little League received a check for $900 toward equipment for the boys' and girls' baseball season. The United Way and Red Cross blood drive both gained Kiwanis support, and oldest member Carl Jones took a bow on his 91st birthday. The member with the longest tenure is Ralph Bisnett, with the club since 1938. Monterey Kiwanis grows and prospers, serving the Monterey Peninsula with its good work.

GREAT MONTEREY SQUID FESTIVAL

In only four short years the Memorial Day weekend has come to mean a time for squid—some call it calamari—and the Great Monterey Squid Festival to residents of the Peninsula. In 1984, when the Monterey Kiwanis inaugurated this fund raiser, they weren't prepared for the enthusiastic passage of 22,000 squid-loving folks through the turnstiles at the Monterey Fairgrounds. They ran out of beer that hot afternoon, and had to have truckloads rushed in; eventually, they even ran out of squid itself.

By the following year the Kiwanis were ready for the mob, but the weatherman was less than friendly. Nonetheless, some 16,700 dedicated fans showed up. The third year brought sunny skies and a return of the multitudes. By now the Squid Festival is as much an institution at the fairgrounds as the county fair itself.

The Kiwanis invented the festival to promote Monterey and spotlight the area's fishing industry. Squid is caught in abundance here, and is one of a rare and delicate quality. The idea germinated in 1983, when past president Bob Massaro solicited the help of the Bostrom Corporation, events management specialists, to create a festival unique to Monterey, and which would also be a fund raiser for civic organizations. Unique, it is the only squid festival in the nation.

Over 130 volunteers put in 1,140 hours of work on the 1986 edition of the festival, which raised $26,000 for local nonprofit agencies including Boys and Girls Clubs, Special Olympics, Hospice of the Monterey Peninsula, YMCA, Meals on Wheels, the United Way, the Salvation Army, and Monterey Pony League Baseball. "The money is quickly returned into the community," Massaro says, "and we create an atmosphere in which other nonprofit organizations can operate concessions.

"We planned to bring notoriety to the squid as a unique seafood, and saw the festival as a way to do it," Massaro adds.

But squid is by no means the only attraction of the festival, nor even the only food available there. Three outdoor stages and one indoor auditorium feature music for all generations, mostly by local entertainers. There are marionettes and other stage shows for children, and the Fort Ord band performs. Scientific exhibits include marine life and the history of commercial fishing in Monterey, and special presentations from the Hoskins Marine Station and California Department of Fish and Game. Of the 56 booths at the 1986 festival, 33 were vendors offering food and beverages, while 23 others featured crafts and specialty items.

The Great Monterey Squid Festival has attracted media attention from San Francisco to New York, including *Time* magazine, and gives awards for the best new recipes for squid. There are more ways to enjoy it than most people would think. Find out for yourself on the next Memorial Day weekend!

Patrons

The following individuals, companies, and organizations have made a valuable commitment to the quality of this publication. Windsor Publications and the Monterey History and Art Association gratefully acknowledge their participation in *The Monterey Peninsula: An Enchanted Land*.

The Alpha Language Group, Inc.
Campos Air & Ocean, Inc.*
Carmel Monterey Travel
The Carmel Pine Cone*
Carmel Valley Ranch Resort*
Community Hospital of the Monterey Peninsula*
Peter J. Coniglio
Bert Cutino and Family
Doubletree Hotel*
El Castell Motel
El Estero Car Wash
First Watch Restaurant*
Flor de Monterey Florist
Geyer Construction, Inc.*
Col. Thomas Duncan Gillis
Great Monterey Squid Festival*
Harbor Realty
Highlands Inn*
Huey and Hudson, Certified Public Accountants
Kirby Low Iron Works
Kiwanis Club of Monterey*
Ruth and Daun La Grange
Mr. and Mrs. R.T. LeFevre

McCord & Wald*
Mildred D. Mendia
Ted W. Minnis, AIA Architect
Monterey Bay Tribune*
Monterey Federal Credit Union*
The Monterey Hotel
Monterey Sand Co.
National Pro-Am Youth Fund*
Office Products, Inc.
Old Capitol Books
Patricia Holman O'Meara
Pebble Beach Company*
Charles George Rudkin
Sardine Factory Restaurant*
Bert Saunders Real Estate
Assemblyman and Mrs. Eric Seastrand
Sparolini Distributing Co.
Otis R. Stevenson DBA Otis Auto Sales
Robert Talbott Ties, Inc.*
Wilma P. Titgen
J.O. Tostevin
USA Hosts Monterey*
Estate of T.A. Work
Yates, Downer, Dyer & Kirkpatrick, Inc.
Eleanore Ziel

*Partners in Progress of *The Monterey Peninsula: An Enchanted Land*. The histories of these companies and organizations appear in Chapter five, beginning on page 99.

Bibliography

"A Retreat By The Sea," *This Month* magazine, January, 1978.

Bancroft, Hubert Howe. *Bancroft's Works.* San Francisco: A.L. Bancroft and Company, 1884.

Beck, Warren A., and Haase, Ynez D. *Historical Atlas of California.* 2nd Printing. Norman, Oklahoma: University of Oklahoma Press, 1975.

Boone, Laurie, and others. *Architecture of The Monterey Peninsula.* Salinas: Monterey Peninsula Museum of Art, 1976.

Bostick, Daisy. *Carmel Today and Yesterday.* Carmel: The Seven Arts, 1945.

Bullock, Wynn, and O'Donnell, Mayo Hayes. *Monterey's Adobe Heritage.* 2nd Printing. Monterey: Monterey Savings and Loan Association, 1968.

Carmel Business Association. *Guide To Carmel-by-the-Sea.* Carmel: Carmel Business Association, 1982.

Colton, Rev. Walter. *Three Years in California.* Palo Alto: Stanford University Press, 1949.

Crouch, Steve. *Fog and Sun Sea and Stone.* Portland, Oregon: Graphic Arts Center Publishing Company, 1980.

Dana, Richard H., Jr. *Two Years Before the Mast.* New York: Dodd, Mead & Company, Inc. 1946.

Davenport, William. *The Monterey Peninsula.* Menlo Park, California: Lane Books, 1965.

Delkin, James Ladd. *Monterey Peninsula.* 2nd ed. Palo Alto: Stanford University, 1946.

Devlin, Robert T. *Pebble Beach, A Matter of Style.* Costa Mesa, California: The Newport Press, 1980.

Dutton, Davis and Judy. *Tales of Monterey.* New York: Ballantine Books, 1974.

Elstob, Winston. *Old Cannery Row.* Orinda, California: Condor's Sky Press and Turtle's Quill Scriptorium, 1965.

Field, Maria Antonia. *California Speaking.* San Francisco: Recorder Printing and Publishing Company, 1914.

Fink, Augusta. *Monterey: The Presence of the Past.* San Francisco: Chronicle Books, 1972.

Fisher, Anne B. *No More A Stranger.* Palo Alto: Stanford University Press, 1946.

Ford, Tirey L. *Dawn and the Dons.* San Francisco: A.M. Robertson, 1926.

Geiger, Maynard, O.F.M. *Franciscan Missionaries in Hispanic California, 1796-1848.* San Marino, California: Huntington Library, 1969.

Hale, Sharron Lee. *A Tribute To Yesterday.* Santa Cruz, California: Valley Publishers, 1980.

Hicks, John and Regina. *Cannery Row, A Pictorial History.* Salinas: I&M Enterprises, 1972.

Hoover, Mildred Brooks, and others. *Historic Spots in California.* 3rd ed., revised by William N. Abeloe. Palo Alto: Stanford University Press, 1970.

Horne, Kibbey M. *A History of the Presidio of Monterey.* Monterey: Presidio of Monterey, 1970.

Hotel Del Monte. San Francisco: Sunset Press, 1899.

Johnson, Robert B. *Old Monterey County: A Pictorial History.* Monterey: Monterey Savings and Loan Association, 1970.

Kingman, Russ. *A Pictorial Life of Jack London.* New York: Crown Publishers, Inc., 1979.

Larkey, Francis B. "Footnotes to the History of the Del Monte Forest." In *Forest Heritage: A Natural History of the Del Monte Forest.* 2nd Printing. Pebble Beach: Del Monte Forest Foundation, 1980.

Lewis, Betty. *Monterey Bay Yesterday.* Fresno: Valley Publishers: 1977.

Lucido, Jerome. *The Italian Heritage of the Monterey Peninsula.* Monterey: The Italian Heritage Society of the Monterey Peninsula, 1979.

Lydon, Sandy. *Chinese Gold.* Capitola, California: Capitola Book Company, 1985.

MacFarland, Grace. *Monterey, Cradle of California's Romance.* Monterey: Weybret Lee Company, 1914.

McLane, Lucy Neely. *A Piney Paradise By Monterey Bay.* 2nd ed. Fresno: Academy Library Guild, 1958.

Miller, Evelyn Grantham, and others, eds. *Pacific Grove, California—The First 100 Years: A Glimpse of the Past That Shapes the City's Present.* Pacific Grove: Centennial, Inc. 1975.

Pacific Grove: An Early Seaside Retreat Revisited. Pacific Grove: City of Pacific Grove, 1978.

Past Present Future California: Information Almanac. Lakewood, California: California Almanac Company, 1969.

Reese, Robert W. *A Brief History of Old Monterey.* Monterey: City of Monterey, 1969.

Reinstedt, Randall A. *Incredible Ghosts of old Monterey's Hotel Del Monte.* Carmel: Ghost Town Publications, 1980.

———— *Portraits of the Past.* Monterey: Monterey Savings and Loan Association, 1979.

———— *Tales, Treasures and Pirates of old Monterey.* Carmel: Ghost Town Publications, 1976.

———— *Where Have All The Sardines Gone?* Carmel: Ghost Town Publications, 1978.

Rolle, Andrew F. *California: A History.* 4th Printing. New York: Thomas Y. Crowell Company, 1966.

Roop, William, and others. *Archaeologist Test Excavations; at 4-Mnt-104 on the property of Hopkins Marine Laboratory, Pacific Grove, Monterey County.* Archaeological Resource Service, 1977.

Scott, Edward B. *A Time for Recollection.* 1st ed. Lake Tahoe, Nevada: Sierra-Tahoe Publishing Company, 1969.

State of California—The Resource Agency. *Monterey State Historic Park; Preliminary General Plan.* Sacramento: State of California—Department of Parks and Recreation, 1981.

Stevenson, Robert Louis. *The Old Pacific Capital.* Monterey: Monterey History and Art Association, 1956.

Sullivan, Colleen, and Finocchi, Mary Ann. *Viejo Monterey.* Monterey: D'Angelo Publishing Company, 1969.

What's Doing magazine. Vol. 3, No. 4. July 1948 (entire issue).

The World Book Encyclopedia. Chicago: Field Enterprises Educational Corporation, 1966.

Considerable information has also been gained from past issues of the following newspapers:

Carmel Pine Cone

Coasting

Monterey Peninsula Herald

Pacific Grove Tribune

The Review

Index

PARTNERS IN PROGRESS INDEX

Campos Air & Ocean, Inc., 110
The Carmel Pine Cone, 121
Carmel Valley Ranch Resort, 118
Community Hospital of the Monterey
    Peninsula, 106-107
Doubletree Hotel, 120
First Watch Restaurant, 116
Geyer Construction, Inc., 114-115
Great Monterey Squid Festival, 123
Highlands Inn, 102
Kiwanis Club of Monterey, 122
McCord & Wald, 117
Monterey Bay Tribune, 119
Monterey Federal Credit Union, 101
Monterey History and Art Association,
    100
National Pro-Am Youth Fund, 103
Pebble Beach Company, 112-113
Sardine Factory Restaurant, 108-109
Talbott Ties, Inc., Robert, 104-105
USA Hosts Monterey, 111

GENERAL INDEX

Italicized numbers indicate illustrations.

Alvarado, Juan Bautista, 20
Alvarado Street, 29
Architecture (Carmel), 78, 78-79
Artists' community, 69-72
Ascension, Antonio de la, 13
Asilomar Conference Grounds, 58, 59
AT&T Pebble Beach National Pro-Am
    Tournament, 95
Austin, Mary, 69, 70

Barreto, Fabian, 89
Barreto, Maria Del Carmen, 89
Bechdolt, Fred, 73
"Big Four" (railroad barons), 26, 55, 90
Booth, Frank E., 28, 29
Borica, Diego de, 16
Bouchard, Hippolyte, 13
Butterfly Parade, 61

Cabrillo, Juan Rodriguez, 41
"California bank notes." *See* Hide and
    tallow trade
California Conference of the Methodist
    Church, 48
California constitutional convention, 21
Californian (newspaper), 20, 21
California State Amateur Golf Cham-
    pionships, 28
Calle Principal, 24

Canary Cottage, 96
Cannery Row, 22, 28, 31, 33, 39
Canning industry, 29, 30, 32, 37
Carmel Bach Festival, 75
Carmel Beach, 86
Carmel Beach House, 77
Carmel Development Company, 69
Carmel Music Society, 74
Carmel *Pine Cone* (newspaper), 80
Carmel River, 13, 76
Carmel Unified School District, 72
Carmel Volunteer Fire Department, 98
Carnegie Coastal Laboratory, 71
Casa Estrada Adobe, 17
Casanova, Angelo, 65
Castillo, El, 16, 36
Central Pacific Railroad, 24
Centrella Hotel, 50
Chautauqua Society, 43, 48, 60
Chinese, 22, 22, 45, 60, 92
City Forestry Commission (Carmel), 71
Coast Guard, 36
Colton, Walter D., 10, 20, 21
Colton Hall, 11, 21
Comstock, Hugh, 79
Congregational Church, 49
Crespi, Juan, 65
Crocker, Charles, 26
Crosby, Bing, 95
Custom House, 19
Cypress Point Clubhouse, 5
Cypress Point Golf Club, 95
Cypress trees, 90

Davenport, J.P., 22
Davis Cup, 28
De Anza, Juan Bautista, 16
Defense Language Institute, 36
Del Mar Hotel, 50, 51
Del Monte Express, 26, 52. *See also*
    Southern Pacific Railroad
Del Monte Forest, 89, 92-93, 93
Del Monte Golf Course, 27
Del Monte Kennel Club Dog Show, 96
Del Monte Properties Company, 31, 94
Del Monte Wave (newspaper), 49, 56
Depression, Great, 32, 58, 97
Devendorf, Frank, 69, 69
Dickinson, Gallant, 20
Dorr, Ebenezer, 13
Duckworth, Santiago J., 65, 66

Eastwood, Clint, 80
Escolle, Honore, 67
Estrada, Jose Mariano, 17
Estrada, Rafael, 19

Feast of Lanterns, 54, 60
Ferrante, Pietro, 29
First Christian Church of Pacific Grove, 49
First Theater, 23
Fisherman's Wharf, 8, 32, 37, 81-82, 83
Fishing industry, 28, 29, 31, 34. *See also*
    Sardine industry
Ford's Department Store, 59
Forest Theater, 70
Fort Ord, 36
Foster, Clarendon E., 56

Golden Bough, The, 75, 76
Gosbey, J.F., 50
Gosby House Inn, 50

Halleck, Henry W., 24
Hammond, Harriet (Mrs. Cyrus McCor-
    mick), 48
Heron, Herbert (Bert), 69
Hide and tallow trade, 17, 19
Highway 1, 33, 35
Holman, R.L. (Luther), 58
Holman, Wilford R., 58
Holman house, 59
Holman's Department Store, 58, 58, 59
Holman family philanthropic activity, 59
Hopkins, Timothy, 55
Hopkins Marine Station of Stanford
    University, 55
Hopkins Seaside Laboratory, 53, 53-54, 55
Hopper, James, 73
Hotel Carmel, 68
Hotel Del Monte, 26, 26, 27, 27, 28,
    30, 31, 32, 36, 39, 49, 50, 56, 90,
    92, 94
Hotel El Carmelo, 49, 49, 50, 50, 52, 58
Hotel San Carlos, 30
House of Four Winds, 24
Hovden, Knute, 29, 31
Hunter, Abbie Jane, 67

Jacks, David, 26, 28, 41, 42, 43, 48, 49,
    90; houses built by, 48
Jacks family, 36
Jeffers, Robinson, 74
Johnson, J.O., 40, 51
Jones, Thomas ap Catesby, 15, 20, 21
Jordan, David Starr, 55, 69

Kuster, Edward G. (Ted), 75, 76; house
    of, 76

Laguna Seca Racetrack, 96
Langford, Benjamin J., 45; house of, 46
La Porte building, 25

Larkin, Thomas Oliver, 23, 24
Larkin House, 23, *24*
Lasuen, Fermin Francisco de, 16, 65
Lewis, Sinclair, 80
Lodge at Pebble Beach, *95, 96*
London, Jack, 70
Lone Cypress, 88
Lopez, Julian, 65
Los Burros Mining District, 24
Lover's Point, *52*, 54, 55, *56*, 58, 60,
    61; Japanese Tea Garden, *54*; bath-
    house at, 56

McDougall, Mattie, 56, 57
McKinley, William, *47*, 49
McLane, Lucy Neely, 45, 58
Macomber, A. Kingsley, 97
Macomber Mansion, *96*, 97
Mammoth Stable, 51, *52*
Methodists, 24, 42, 43, 48, 65
Mexican era of Monterey, 16, 19, 21
Mexican War, 21
Mission San Carlos Borromeo del Rio
    Carmelo, 6, 12, 13, 16, *62*, 64, 65, 66
Monarch butterflies, 41, 61, 86; parade
    in honor of, *61*
Monterey and Pacific Grove Street Rail-
    way, *51*, 52
Monterey and Salinas Valley Railroad, 24
Monterey Bay Aquarium, 38, *85*
Monterey Conference Center, 38-39, *39*
Monte Rey, Count de, 11
Monterey County Symphony, 75
Monterey History and Art Association,
    23, 32
Monterey Peninsula Country Club, 94
Monterey Peninsula Herald (newspaper), 35
Monterey Peninsula Orchestra Associa-
    tion, 75
Morgan, Julia, 59
Morse, Samuel F.B., 32, 36, *94*, 94, 97
Mount Carmel, 64
Municipal Wharf Number One. *See*
    Fisherman's Wharf
Municipal Wharf Number Two, 32, *36*
Murray, James, 28
Murray Mansion, 28

Naval Postgraduate School, 36
Neve, Felipe de, 16
Neville, Jack, 94
Newberry, Perry, 80

Oldfield, Barney, 28
Osbourne, Fanny, 25

Pacific Grove Hotel, 58. *See also* Hotel
    El Carmelo
Pacific Grove Marine Gardens, 61
Pacific Grove Methodist Church, 51
Pacific Grove Retreat, *42, 43*, 43, *44*,
    47; "blue laws" of, 44-45
Pacific Grove Retreat Association, 43, 49
Pacific Grove Review (newspaper), 54, 69
Pacific Improvement Company, 26, 49,
    54, 55, 56, 57, 59, 90, 94
Palou, Francisco, 64
Pebble Beach Concours d'Elegance, 96
Pebble Beach Dressage Championships, 96
Pebble Beach Equestrian Center, 96
Pebble Beach Lodge, 50
Pebble Beach Road Races, 95
Pebble Beach Summer Horse Show, 96
Peck, Jesse Truesdale, 42, 43
Perkins, Hayes, 4, 60, 61
Perkins Park, *2-3*, 4, 60
Perouse, Comte de la, 13
Pescadero, El, 89, 90, 92
Pine Inn, *70*, 71
Platt, Julia B., 56, 57, 58
Point Cabrillo, 55
Point Pinos, 41, 43, 44
Point Pinos Lighthouse, *42*
Portola, Gaspar de, 12, 13
Powers, Frank H., 69
Presidio, 13, 16, 36
Punta de Pinos, 89

Roberts, John L.D., 33, 35
Ross, Reverend, 42, 43
Royal Presidio Chapel, *12*, 14, 65
Ruiz, Manuel, 14
Russian exploration, 12, 15

St. Mary's-by-the-Sea Episcopal

Church, 46, 48
Salgo, Sandor, *75*
Salinas Weekly Register (newspaper), 67
San Carlos Cathedral, 14, 67
San Diego, 19
Sardine industry, 29, 31, 33, *34*, 35, *38*.
    See also Fishing industry
Scribner's Magazine, 69
Semple, Robert, 20, 21
Serra, Junipero, 6, *12*, 13, 14, 29, 63,
    64, 65, *65*
Seventeen Mile Drive, 28, *90*, 90, *91*, 92
Sherman, William T., 24
Sherman Adobe, 24
Sloat, John Drake, 19, 21
Smith, William, 56
Soberanes Adobe, *19*
Sola, Pablo Vincente, 16
Southern Pacific Railroad, 24, 26, 52,
    54, 65
Spyglass Hill Golf Links, 95
Steinbeck, John, 38
Sterling, George, 69, *70*, 70
Stevenson, Robert Louis, 25, 43, 45,
    64, 65, 90
Stevenson House, Robert Louis, *25*
Stillwater Cove, 92
Swan, Jack, 23

Tourist industry; in Monterey, 38-39,
    59-60; in Carmel, 76-78

U.S. interest in Monterey, 20, 21

Vancouver, George, 13
Vizcaino, Sebastian, 11, 12, 13, 64

Whaling industry, 22
Williams, Michael, *73*
Witch Tree, *84*
Women's Real Estate Investment Com-
    pany, 67, 69
World War I Memorial Arch (Carmel), *72*
World War II, 35, 36
W.R. Holman Highway, 58

Mary Anis Bishop Oliver stands in the doorway of the Custom
House Art Emporium in the late 1890s. Her husband, Joseph
Kurtz Oliver, opened the curio shop in 1896. In 1903 Oliver tore
down the store and replaced it with a two-story building, the
downstairs portion housing the curio shop for more than 50 years.
This area is now a part of the Custom House Plaza. Courtesy,
Monterey Savings and Loan Association